WAYS TO IMPROVE YOUR BRIDGE

f you are a middle of the road player keen to advance, this book will
how you the way forward.

David Bird has taken ten key areas in bidding and play, applying
considerable skills as a player and critic to prove how better
ts can be gained. The topics range from bidding the opponents'
it, managing trumps, and battling for the part-score, to directing
opening lead, support doubles and re-doubles, and splinter bids
nd fit jumps. The essential points to remember are summarised at
e nd of each chapter and there are problems to solve which will
how you how much you have taken on board.

hy wait any longer? – your opportunity to become a better player
re!

* * *

d Bird, recognised as the world's leading humorous bridge
er who combines wit and wisdom in equal measure, is also a
er of distinction. He is, furthermore, the bridge critic for the
ndon *Evening Standard*, the *Mail on Sunday* and the *Glasgow
ening Times*.

TEN WAYS TO IMPROVE YOUR BRIDGE

David Bird

CASSELL
IN ASSOCIATION WITH
PETER CRAWLEY

First published in Great Britain 2000
in association with Peter Crawley
by Victor Gollancz
Second impression 2004
published in association with Peter Crawley
by Cassell
Wellington House, 125 Strand, London WC2R 0BB
a division of the Orion Publishing Group Ltd

A catalogue record for this book is available from the
British Library

ISBN 0-304-36674-9

Typeset at The Spartan Press Ltd,
Lymington, Hants

Printed in Great Britain by
Clays Ltd, St Ives plc

Contents

1. Bidding the Opponents' Suit

You may be surprised to hear that around half the bridge players in the world make no use at all of bids in a suit called by the opponents. They complete their auctions with bids in the remaining three suits, or in no-trumps. Any suggestion as to how they might make good use of a bid in the opponents' suit is regarded as somehow improper. 'We don't like to do that at our club . . .'

A bid in the opponents' suit, known as a cue-bid, is immensely useful. Its most common meaning is that you have a good hand of some sort and in this chapter we will explore the various situations in which such a bid can be made. If you have not used these bids before, you will be amazed how much more accurate your competitive bidding becomes.

A cue-bid facing a take-out double

One simple use of a strength-showing bid in the opponents' suit arises when you are responding to a take-out double. Imagine the auction starts like this:

West	North	East	South
1◇	Dble	Pass	?

Sitting South, you should reply along these general lines:

   0–7 points: bid your longest suit at the minimum level
   8–11 points: jump in your longest suit
   12+ points: bid game or cue-bid opponents' suit (here 2◇)

Suppose, as South, you hold one of these hands:

(1)	♠ A Q 9 4	(2)	♠ K 10 9 6 3	(3)	♠ A J 4
	♡ K J 6 2		♡ A Q 10 8 3		◇ Q 10 8
	◇ A 8 6		◇ J 5		◇ 9 5
	♣ 7 6		♣ 4		♣ A Q J 8 4

On (1) you want to be in game but do not know which game. You pass this message with a cue-bid of 2◇. Those players who regard such an action as too esoteric will have to guess which major-suit game to bid. Often they will end in a 4–3 fit. Once you have shown your strength with a cue-bid, the bidding continues naturally and any 4–4 fit in a major will come to light.

Hand (2) is easily strong enough for game, facing a take-out double. Again you cannot be sure of the best game, so you begin by showing your power with a cue-bid of 2◇. The same is true with (3). A jump response of 3♣ would be non-forcing. It would show a hand in the middle (8–11) range and partner would often then pass. Instead, you should cue-bid 2◇. Partner will doubtless bid one of the majors and you will continue with 3♣, now forcing. You hope that partner has a diamond stopper and can bid 3NT.

The bidding will usually reach game after a cue-bid response, but it doesn't have to. Most partnerships treat a cue-bid response as 'forcing to suit agreement'. In other words the auction can stop after a bid by either player has been raised:

West	North	East	South		WEST	EAST
–	1◇	Dble	Pass		♠ A J 7 6	♠ K Q 8 2
2◇	Pass	2♡	Pass		♡ K 10 7 5	♡ A 9 6 3
3♡	End				◇ 9 8 4	◇ J 3
					♣ K 2	♣ Q J 4

Here East has a minimum take-out double. He passes the single raise and avoids reaching a near-hopeless game.

A cue-bid facing an overcall

One of the main reasons for overcalling is to remove bidding space from the opponents. Suppose the bidding starts like this:

West	North	East	South
1♣	1♠		

North's overcall has made East's task in responding more difficult. He cannot respond 1◇ or 1♡ and if he responds 2◇ or 2♡ instead, the bidding will have reached an uncomfortably high level in a short time.

Since the removal of bidding space causes so many problems for the opponents, you should aim to raise partner's overcall whenever possible.

West	North	East	South	SOUTH
1♣	1♠	Pass	?	♠ Q 7 4
				♡ J 9 6 3
				◇ K 10 7 2
				♣ 9 5

Your hand does not amount to much and the chance of making game is minimal. Nevertheless you should raise to 2♠, whatever the vulnerability. The opener is likely to hold a strong hand and will be greatly incapacitated if you remove 1NT and all the two-level bids from his armoury.

With 4-card support for partner's overcall you can make an even greater nuisance of yourself:

West	North	East	South	SOUTH
1♣	1♠	Pass	?	♠ K 7 4 3
				♡ J 9
				◇ A 10 7 6 2
				♣ 9 5

Now you should raise, pre-emptively, to 3♠. The opener, who may well be looking at some promising 18-count, will not like the sound of your raise at all! He will either have to pass or risk coming in again at a very high level, perhaps to suffer a big penalty when your partner is relatively strong. You would make the same raise to 3♠ if East had entered the auction – perhaps raising to 2♣ or making a negative (take-out) double.

If direct raises of partner's suit are used for pre-emptive effect, you must use some different bid when there is a genuine prospect of game. Any idea what this might be?

To show a hand with strong support, responder will (you guessed it) cue-bid the opener's suit.

West	North	East	South	SOUTH
1♣	1♠	Pass	?	♠ A J 4 3
				♡ K 6
				◇ A 10 7 2
				♣ 9 5 4

You bid 2♣ on the South cards. This promises fair strength (at least 9 points) and shows a sound raise to 2♠ at least. If partner rebids only 2♠, this will mean that he has a minimum overcall and rates game as unlikely. With this particular hand you would then pass. Give yourself another king or queen and you would try again by raising to 3♠.

You see the advantage of this scheme? When partner overcalls, you can make two types of raise: pre-emptive and constructive. Those who regard the bidding of the opponents' suit as beyond their compass will be losing out in one area or another.

A cue-bid facing an opening bid

We saw in the last section that you should aim to remove bidding space from the opponents when you have a good fit for partner's overcall. This idea applies with equal force when partner has opened the bidding and an opponent has overcalled. Suppose you are East here:

West	North	East	South	EAST
1♡	2♣	?		♠ 4 3
				♡ A J 9 4
				◇ 10 8 7 6 2
				♣ 5 4

There's a good chance that the opponents have a spade fit and you would like to shut them out by jumping to 3♡. You can! Once an opponent has overcalled, you should play a jump raise to 3♡ as pre-emptive. With a genuine (game-try) raise to the three level you would cue-bid the opponents' suit instead:

West	North	East	South	EAST
1♡	2♣ ·	?		♠ K 9 3
				♡ K J 9 4
				◇ A 10 4 3
				♣ 9 3

Holding those East cards, you can see genuine chances of a heart game. You cue-bid 3♣, showing a sound (rather than pre-emptive) raise to the three-level or higher. If partner rebids only 3♡, declining your invitation, you will pass.

Cue-bid facing a 'short minor' opening

Some of you will play a strong 1NT opening and therefore have to open 1♣ or 1♢ on suits of less than four cards. Although responder will not normally raise such an opening unless he has at least 5-card support, this does not alter at all the relative meanings of a jump raise and a cue-bid:

West	North	East	South		EAST
1♣ (1)	1♡	?		♠	9 7
				♡	8 6
(1) May be short				♢	J 10 7 3
				♣	A J 9 3 2

Raise to 3♣. This may block out an enemy spade fit. It will also reduce South's options, should he want to raise the hearts. Partner will not place you with a genuine game-try because if your hand were stronger, you would cue-bid instead:

West	North	East	South		EAST
1♣ (1)	1♡	?		♠	K 10 3
				♡	8 6
(1) May be short				♢	J 10 7
				♣	A K 9 3 2

East bids 2♡, showing 5-card club support and the values for a sound game-try, at least.

A cue-bid by the opener

As we have seen, a cue-bid in the opponents' suit usually carries the meaning 'I am strong'. The opener should resort to such an action only when he does not have a more descriptive call available.

West	North	East	South		WEST
1♢	1♡	1♠	Pass	♠	3
?				♡	A 6
				♢	A K 10 9 6
				♣	A Q J 5 4

It would be wrong to cue-bid 2♡ here, just because you are strong. A jump to 3♣ paints a clearer picture.

The same is true when you have 4-card support for responder:

West	North	East	South		WEST
1♢	1♡	1♠	Pass	♠	A 10 5 4
?				♡	K 6
				♢	A Q J 9 2
				♣	K 4

A jump to 4♠ expresses the hand well. There is no point in a cue-bid when you have a descriptive natural bid available.

You would use a cue-bid on this type of hand:

West	North	East	South		WEST
1♢	1♡	1♠	Pass	♠	K 5
?				♡	8 6
				♢	A K Q 9 7 5 2
				♣	A Q

Too strong to rebid 3♢, you indicate a powerful hand by cue-bidding 2♡. When the wind is in your direction, partner may be able to bid no-trumps. He may instead rebid his spades, allowing you to play in that suit. If he bids an unhelpful 3♣, you will bid 3♢ – forcing when preceded by a cue-bid.

A cue-bid following a take-out double

We have already seen that the responder to a take-out double can show strength by making a cue-bid. The same applies to the doubler himself.

West	North	East	South		NORTH
1♢	Dble	Pass	2♣	♠	A K J 4
Pass	?			♡	A K 8
				♢	8 6
				♣	A Q 9 2

With 21 points, you are too strong for a raise to 3♣. Your best move is a cue-bid of 2♢. In the unlikely event that partner bids spades now, you can raise to game in that suit. If instead partner bids 2♡ or 2NT, you will bid 3♣ next, having already indicated a very strong hand.

What if South rebids 3♣ himself? You would then have to choose between a cautious Pass or (my choice) a raise to 4♣.

Again, do not opt for the cue-bid when you have a descriptive alternative available.

West	North	East	South		NORTH
1♢	Dble	Pass	1♠	♠	A K J 4
Pass	?			♡	A 8
				♢	8 6
				♣	A Q 10 9 3

You are just about worth 4♠. If you think not, make it 3♠. There is nothing to be gained by a cue-bid of 2♢, anyway!

Michaels cue-bids

Your right-hand opponent opens 1♢. What meaning should be attached to an immediate overcall of 2♢?

In the early days of bridge, a cue-bid overcall was used to show an unusually strong take-out double. This was a poor idea. It wasted space and made it more difficult for partner to show any values that he might hold. Nowadays, nearly all tournament players use a cue-bid to show a two-suited hand. The most popular method is the Michaels cue-bid:

Over 1♣ or 1♢, a cue-bid shows both majors.
Over 1♡ or 1♠, a cue-bid shows the other major and a minor.

These hands represent typical Michaels cue-bids:

	(1)	♠ A Q 8 4 3	(2)	♠ A J 9 7 3
		♡ K 10 7 6 2		♡ A K 10 9 7 3
		♢ 7 4		♢ 2
		♣ 6		♣ A

On both hands you would bid 2♣ over an opening of 1♣, or 2♢ over 1♢. The hand does not need to be strong, as you see from (1). When you have considerable power in reserve, as in (2), you will make a further bid over partner's response. If partner responds 2♠ you will continue with 3♡, showing extra strength and longer hearts than spades. If instead partner responded 2♡, you would raise to game in hearts.

Suppose, now, that your right-hand opponent has opened 1♡ and you hold one of these hands:

(3)	♠ K Q 9 7 6	(4)	♠ K 10 8 7 3	(5)	♠ K J 8 7 5 3
	♡ 9 3		♡ 7		♡ 4
	◇ 2		◇ A Q 9 7 4 2		◇ K J 10 7 4
	♣ K J 9 7 2		♣ 5		♣ Q

With (3) you would bid a Michaels 2♡. If partner does not hold 3-card spade support, but does hold at least three cards in each minor, he can bid 2NT to ask which minor suit you hold. A Michaels 2♡ would be fine on hand (4), too. When you hold six cards in the unbid major, as in (5), it is better tactics to overcall in the major (here, 1♠). Facing a Michaels bid, partner would head for your minor on such as 2-5-3-3 shape. You would be better off playing in spades, one level lower.

A Michaels cue-bid applies in fourth seat too (for example, 1♡ – Pass – Pass – 2♡). It may be used also when there has been a 1NT response (1◇ – Pass – 1NT – 2◇).

How do you respond to a Michaels cue-bid? It's similar to responding to an overcall. You can make pre-emptive raises in one of the indicated suits, or show genuine game interest in one of the suits by making a further cue-bid yourself.

West	North	East	South	WEST	EAST
–	–	–	1♣	♠ A Q 9 7 3	♠ K J 6 4
2♣	Pass	3♠	End	♡ K Q 7 5 2	♡ 8 3
				◇ 8 6	◇ J 9 7 2
				♣ 2	♣ Q 8 4

North–South can probably make at least 10 tricks in clubs, but East's pre-emptive 3♠ may well buy the contract. Since West is relatively strong, 3♠ is likely to succeed on this occasion.

West	North	East	South	WEST	EAST
–	–	–	1♣	♠ A Q 9 7 3	♠ A 10 6 4
2♣	Pass	3♣	Pass	♡ K Q 7 5 2	♡ J 3
4♡	Pass	4♠	End	◇ 8 6	◇ A 9 7 3
				♣ 2	♣ Q 8 4

Here East is stronger and can see genuine chances of game. He indicates this with a cue-bid of 3♣ (not yet letting West know which trump suit he has in mind). With a minimum hand West would sign off in 3♡. Here he accepts with 4♡ and East corrects to 4♠.

Natural bids in an opponent's suit

What do you do when you have a long and strong holding in a suit bid naturally by an opponent? When the opening is on your right, you must pass initially.

West	North	East	South	NORTH
1♡	?			♠ 6 4
				♡ A Q J 9 7 2
				◇ 8 3
				♣ K Q 4

You pass on the first round, leaving yourself the option of bidding 2♡ (natural) at your next turn.

The situation is different when you are in the fourth seat and the opponents have bid two suits, including the one where you are strong:

West	North	East	South	NORTH
–	–	1♣	Pass	♠ A K Q 9 8 4
1♠	?			♡ A 6 2
				◇ 3
				♣ J 10 5

If you held a red two-suiter, you could double now (or bid an Unusual 2NT if your distribution was exceptional). The bids of 2♣ and 2♠ are therefore available in a natural sense. Here you would bid 2♠, telling partner that your spades were worth a mention even after West's response in the suit. Switch the black suits and you would overcall 2♣, again a natural bid.

POINTS TO REMEMBER

1. A bid in the opponents' suit is a useful weapon in competitive auctions. Its most frequent meaning is to show strength.
2. Facing a take-out double, a cue-bid shows game values (or thereabouts) but doubt about which game will be best.

3. Facing an overcall, or an opening bid that has been overcalled, a cue-bid shows a sound raise (rather than a pre-emptive raise).

4. When you have a good fit (4-card or better) for an opening bid or overcall, make a jump raise whenever possible. Partner will not expect a strong hand, because you would then have made a cue-bid instead.

5. When the opener, or a player who has made a take-out double, subsequently makes a cue-bid, he shows a strong hand with no satisfactory natural bid to make.

TEST YOURSELF

A. Your left-hand opponent opens 1♡ and partner makes a take-out double. If you respond 2♠ to the double, what sort of hand will this show?

B. The opponent on your right opens 1◇. You make a take-out double and the next player passes. What does it mean when your partner responds 2◇?

C. Your partner doubles 1♣, the next player passing. What would you respond on these hands:

(1) ♠ A Q 8 4 3	(2) ♠ K 10 8 7	(3) ♠ J 4 2
♡ 7 2	♡ A Q 10 7 4	♡ K Q 9 4
◇ Q 4 3	◇ 9 2	◇ A Q 8 6 3
♣ 9 8 4	♣ A 5	♣ 9

D. When partner has overcalled, what is the purpose of responding with a cue-bid in the opponents' suit (a sequence such as 1◇ – 1♠ – Pass – 2◇)?

E. Your left-hand opponent opens 1◇ and partner overcalls 1♠, the next player passing. What would you say on these hands:

	(1)		(2)		(3)
♠	Q 10 5	♠	K Q 8 7 2	♠	A J 4
♡	7 2	♡	7	♡	A 10 9 4
◇	10 9 4 3	◇	9 5 2	◇	8 6
♣	K J 7 3	♣	A 10 7 4	♣	K 8 6 3

F. Your left-hand opponent opens 1♡ and partner overcalls 2♡. What type of hand does this show? What would you respond on these hands:

	(1)		(2)		(3)
♠	5	♠	A Q 8 7 2	♠	J 4
♡	Q 9 8 7 3	♡	7	♡	A 10 9 4
◇	J 9 4	◇	K 10 6 3	◇	K J 9 7 3
♣	A 8 6 3	♣	J 7 3	♣	6 2

ANSWERS

A. A jump response to a take-out double suggests 8–11 points. With a stronger hand you would respond with a cue-bid, or leap directly to game.

B. Partner's response shows a strong hand usually of 12 points or more. The bidding will now proceed naturally and game will usually be reached.

C. On hand (1) you should respond 2♠, suggesting a hand of around 8–11 points. Hand (2) justifies a cue-bid response of 2♣, showing 12 points or more. If partner continues with 2♠, you will raise to 4♠ (a single raise to 3♠ would be non-forcing). Hand (3) is again worth a cue-bid response of 2♣. If partner says 2♠ next, you will rebid 3◇.

D. To show a sound raise of the overcall, rather than a pre-emptive raise.

E. On (1) you should raise to 2♠. This is not a strong bid and partner will realise that you are merely trying to make life difficult for the opener. Hand (2) justifies a pre-emptive raise to 4♠. If the spade game goes down, it is probable that the opponents could have made some contract their way. Hand (3) represents a sound game-try in spades and you should make a cue-bid response of 2◇. If partner rebids only 2♠, showing a minimum overcall, you will pass.

F. Partner's 2♡ is a Michaels cue-bid, showing a two-suiter in spades and one of the minors. On hand (1) you would respond 2NT, asking partner which minor he holds. On (2), with a 5-5 fit in spades, you would jump to 4♠. With hand (3), the chances are high that partner has spades and clubs, rather than spades and diamonds. You would keep as low as possible by responding 2♠.

2. Managing the Trump Suit

You may think you know all there is to know about drawing trumps. Perhaps you do. We will soon see! It's a more complex part of the game than many players realise.

When is it wrong to draw trumps immediately?

How many situations can you think of where it would be wrong to draw trumps immediately, after winning the opening lead? An obvious one is when you need to take some ruffs and cannot afford to remove dummy's trumps. Another may arise when the opening lead has dented your defences in one of the side suits:

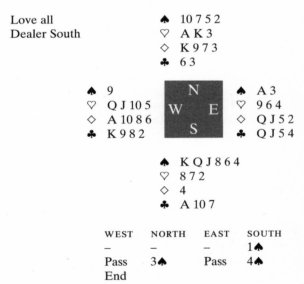

Love all
Dealer South

	♠	10 7 5 2
	♡	A K 3
	♢	K 9 7 3
	♣	6 3

♠	9		♠	A 3
♡	Q J 10 5		♡	9 6 4
♢	A 10 8 6		♢	Q J 5 2
♣	K 9 8 2		♣	Q J 5 4

	♠	K Q J 8 6 4
	♡	8 7 2
	♢	4
	♣	A 10 7

WEST	NORTH	EAST	SOUTH
–	–	–	1♠
Pass	3♠	Pass	4♠
End			

West leads ♡Q against your spade game. It's not difficult to see what will happen if you win the lead and play a trump. The defenders will remove your last heart stopper and you will then lose a trick in each suit.

To avoid this fate, you must try to establish a discard for your heart loser. After winning the heart lead, you should cross to the ace of clubs and lead a diamond towards dummy. Luck is with you on this occasion. West has the ace and you will make the game whether he plays the card on this trick or not.

Sometimes you delay drawing trumps because dummy's last trump will be needed as an entry. That's the situation here:

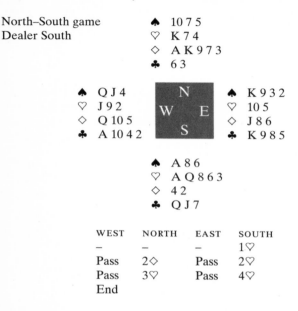

North–South game
Dealer South

♠ 10 7 5
♡ K 7 4
◇ A K 9 7 3
♣ 6 3

♠ Q J 4
♡ J 9 2
◇ Q 10 5
♣ A 10 4 2

♠ K 9 3 2
♡ 10 5
◇ J 8 6
♣ K 9 8 5

♠ A 8 6
♡ A Q 8 6 3
◇ 4 2
♣ Q J 7

WEST	NORTH	EAST	SOUTH
–	–	–	1♡
Pass	2◇	Pass	2♡
Pass	3♡	Pass	4♡
End			

You and your partner overbid somewhat (nothing to be ashamed of!) and reach a poor game. You win the spade-queen lead with the ace and see four black-suit losers staring you in the face. The only hope is that the diamonds break 3-3 and the suit can be established with one ruff. It will not be possible to draw three rounds of trumps before playing on diamonds, because the trump king will be needed as an entry to dummy. You draw two rounds of trumps with the ace and queen (which may save you from an extra undertrick, should the diamonds not break), then cash dummy's top diamonds. A diamond ruff in the South hand brings the good news that the diamonds are indeed 3-3. You can now cross to the king of trumps to enjoy two long cards in the diamond suit. You score four diamonds, five trumps, and the ace of spades. Game made!

How many rounds of trumps should I draw?

There are various situations where you can increase your chances by drawing some of the enemy trumps, but not all. Your general aim will be to leave enough trumps in dummy for ruffing purposes, while minimising the risk of suffering a ruff or overruff by the defenders. Look at this deal:

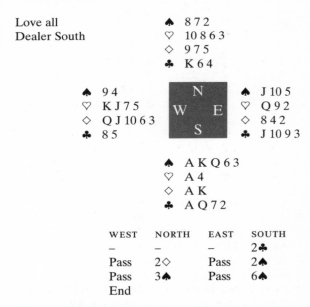

Love all
Dealer South

```
              ♠  8 7 2
              ♡  10 8 6 3
              ◇  9 7 5
              ♣  K 6 4

♠  9 4                        ♠  J 10 5
♡  K J 7 5                    ♡  Q 9 2
◇  Q J 10 6 3                 ◇  8 4 2
♣  8 5                        ♣  J 10 9 3

              ♠  A K Q 6 3
              ♡  A 4
              ◇  A K
              ♣  A Q 7 2
```

WEST	NORTH	EAST	SOUTH
–	–	–	2♣
Pass	2◇	Pass	2♠
Pass	3♠	Pass	6♠
End			

You win West's ◇Q lead and note that there is an unavoidable loser in hearts. To make the slam, you must therefore avoid a club loser. What will happen if your first move is to draw three rounds of trumps? You will go down. Clubs do not break 3-3 and East will retain his club guard.

Suppose instead that you draw no trumps at all, playing on clubs straight away. That's no good either. West will ruff the third round of clubs.

The only way to make the contract is to draw precisely two rounds of trumps. When you then play the three top clubs, West will show out on the third round but will be unable to ruff. The way will be clear for you to ruff your last club with dummy's 8. If West had held three trumps instead of two, you would have gone down. But in that case there would be no way of making the contract.

When the defender who is short in the key side suit does hold the long trumps, you may still succeed. Once he is void in the side suit, you must lead a low card through his hand, towards an honour sitting over him. In that way you ensure that he can ruff only a small card rather than an honour. This deal illustrates the technique:

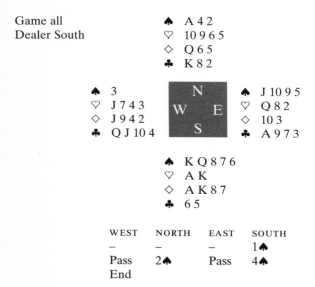

Game all
Dealer South

```
                    ♠ A 4 2
                    ♡ 10 9 6 5
                    ◇ Q 6 5
                    ♣ K 8 2

     ♠ 3                          ♠ J 10 9 5
     ♡ J 7 4 3        N           ♡ Q 8 2
     ◇ J 9 4 2    W       E       ◇ 10 3
     ♣ Q J 10 4       S           ♣ A 9 7 3

                    ♠ K Q 8 7 6
                    ♡ A K
                    ◇ A K 8 7
                    ♣ 6 5
```

WEST	NORTH	EAST	SOUTH
–	–	–	1♠
Pass	2♠	Pass	4♠
End			

With 28 points between the hands you might not expect 4♠ to be a problem. West starts with ♣Q, however, and the defenders play three rounds of the suit, forcing you to ruff. What now? Trumps don't break and you will have to deal with the fourth round of diamonds. How would you continue the play?

You should draw two rounds of trumps with the ace and king, discovering the 4-1 break. Then you play the ace of diamonds, followed by a diamond to the queen. The big moment has arrived. A third round of diamonds is led through East, the defender with the trumps, towards your remaining honour. If East ruffs, it will be the last trick for his side; you will draw the outstanding trump when you regain the lead. Nor does East fare any better by discarding. You will win the trick with the diamond king, then ruff your remaining diamond with dummy's last trump. East is welcome to overruff, since this will consume his natural trump trick.

Suppose instead that you simply play the queen of diamonds, followed by the ace and king. This will not be good enough. East will

ruff the king and with a trick still to be lost in diamonds you will be one
down. It is essential to lead towards your remaining honour, once the
defender is in a position to ruff.

Let's look at a similar, but perhaps more difficult, hand:

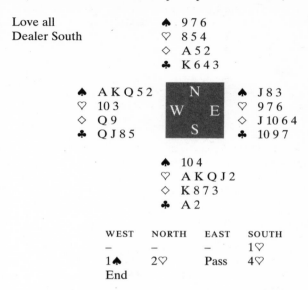

Love all   ♠ 9 7 6
Dealer South   ♡ 8 5 4
         ♢ A 5 2
         ♣ K 6 4 3

♠ A K Q 5 2   ♠ J 8 3
♡ 10 3   ♡ 9 7 6
♢ Q 9   ♢ J 10 6 4
♣ Q J 8 5   ♣ 10 9 7

        ♠ 10 4
        ♡ A K Q J 2
        ♢ K 8 7 3
        ♣ A 2

WEST	NORTH	EAST	SOUTH
–	–	–	1♡
1♠	2♡	Pass	4♡
End			

West launches the defence with his three top spades. You ruff the
third round and see that you must make plans for your fourth
diamond. The village idiot will succeed when diamonds are 3-3. What
can you do when they are 4-2?

Suppose you draw two rounds of trumps, as on the previous hand,
then play ace, king and another diamond. That's no good. The
defender who wins the third round will either play another round of
trumps, removing dummy's last trump, or (if partner has the last
trump) give his partner a diamond ruff.

The potentially dangerous moment will occur when the defenders
take their diamond trick. To prevent them doing any damage, you
should let them win the *first* round of diamonds. At trick 4 you play a
low diamond, allowing West's 9 to win. Suppose West switches to ♣Q
now. You will win with dummy's king, draw two rounds of trumps,
then play the ace and king of diamonds. West shows out but has no
trump with which to ruff. You ruff your last diamond in the dummy,
then return to the ace of clubs to draw East's last trump.

The play would be similar if West chose to return a fourth round of spades. You would ruff in the South hand, draw two rounds of trumps and continue as before. Playing this way still succeeds, of course, when diamonds were 3-3 all along.

Sometimes you have two ruffs to take in the key suit. What do you make of this deal?

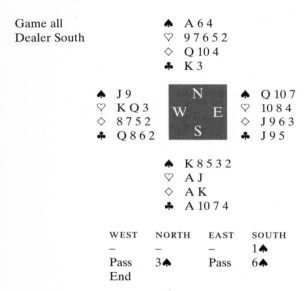

	♠ A 6 4		
Game all	♡ 9 7 6 5 2		
Dealer South	◇ Q 10 4		
	♣ K 3		

WEST	NORTH	EAST	SOUTH
–	–	–	1♠
Pass	3♠	Pass	6♠
End			

You may not think much of the bidding but there are plenty of players (believe me!) who bid like that. How would you tackle the play after West leads ♡K?

Your first priority is to dispose of the heart loser exposed by the lead. You cash the ace and king of diamonds, then cross to the ace of trumps to throw your heart loser on the diamond queen. You play the king and ace of clubs, then ruff a third round of clubs in dummy. You must now ruff the fourth round of clubs, even though you fully expect one of the defenders to be able to ruff with a higher trump than dummy's 6. You hope that the defender who ruffs will do so from the 3-card trump holding.

Here you are in luck. You cross to hand with a heart ruff and ruff your last club in dummy. East overruffs, but in doing so consumes his natural trump trick. You ruff his red-suit return, draw the two out-standing trumps with your king, and score up the slam.

When to concede a master trump

Time for something different. Suppose you have drawn two rounds of trumps and there is one master trump outstanding. In general, there will be little point in playing a further round of trumps. You will expend two trumps, which might have been used for ruffing. An exception arises when dummy has a suit to run and the defender's master trump could be used to interrupt this.

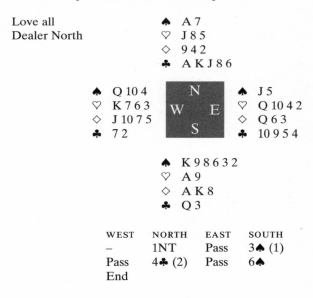

Love all   ♠ A 7
Dealer North   ♡ J 8 5
               ◇ 9 4 2
               ♣ A K J 8 6

♠ Q 10 4   ♠ J 5
♡ K 7 6 3   ♡ Q 10 4 2
◇ J 10 7 5   ◇ Q 6 3
♣ 7 2   ♣ 10 9 5 4

               ♠ K 9 8 6 3 2
               ♡ A 9
               ◇ A K 8
               ♣ Q 3

WEST	NORTH	EAST	SOUTH
–	1NT	Pass	3♠ (1)
Pass	4♣ (2)	Pass	6♠
End			

(1) 6-card suit, suggesting a slam
(2) Cue-bid, showing first-round club control

You arrive in Six Spades and we'll assume first that West leads ◇J. You win with the ace and draw two rounds of trumps with the ace and king, pleased to see them break 3-2. What next? If you play three rounds of clubs, throwing one of your losers, your evening (or afternoon) will be spoilt. West will ruff with the trump queen and – with no entry back to dummy – there will be no way to dispose of your remaining loser. One down!

To make the contract you must play a third round of trumps, conceding a trick to West's master queen. You can then win the return and run the club suit without fear of interruption.

Things would be different if West had struck the best lead of a heart.

You would have to choose between cashing two trumps before turning to the clubs (gaining when the defender with two clubs held two trumps), and cashing only the trump king before turning to clubs (gaining when the defender with two clubs held three trumps). The latter line is slightly better and would succeed here.

(By the way, did anything else occur to you? North can make Seven Clubs, simply by setting up the spade suit! It shows how difficult bidding can be.)

When to duck an early round of trumps

Sometimes you have to choose the right moment to surrender a trump trick which has to be lost. You must lose it at a time when the opponents cannot harm you.

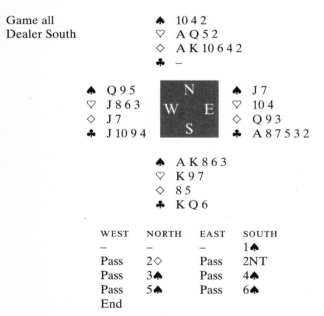

Game all
Dealer South

	♠	10 4 2
	♡	A Q 5 2
	♢	A K 10 6 4 2
	♣	—

♠ Q 9 5	♠ J 7
♡ J 8 6 3	♡ 10 4
♢ J 7	♢ Q 9 3
♣ J 10 9 4	♣ A 8 7 5 3 2

	♠	A K 8 6 3
	♡	K 9 7
	♢	8 5
	♣	K Q 6

WEST	NORTH	EAST	SOUTH
–	–	–	1♠
Pass	2♢	Pass	2NT
Pass	3♠	Pass	4♠
Pass	5♠	Pass	6♠
End			

West leads ♣J and you ruff in the dummy. What next? Suppose you draw two rounds of trumps, then play to set up the diamonds. West will overruff the third round of diamonds and, with no trumps left in the dummy, you will lose a club trick. The same fate awaits if you cross to ♡K and take a second club ruff before playing the top two trumps.

You have to lose a trump trick eventually and it makes good sense to do this at a time when the opponents cannot cash a club. After ruffing the first trick, you should duck a round of trumps – playing a low trump from both hands. The defenders cannot cash a club then because you still have a trump in dummy. Whatever they return, you will win, draw trumps, and set up the diamonds with one ruff. You can then return to dummy with a heart to discard your two remaining clubs on the good diamonds.

You must duck a trump on the next hand, too, although the reason for doing so is different.

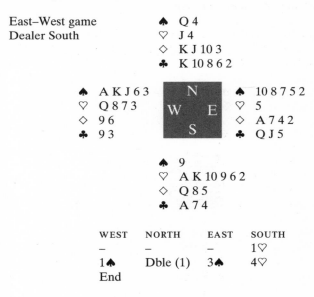

```
East–West game          ♠ Q 4
Dealer South            ♡ J 4
                        ◇ K J 10 3
                        ♣ K 10 8 6 2

        ♠ A K J 6 3         N          ♠ 10 8 7 5 2
        ♡ Q 8 7 3       W       E      ♡ 5
        ◇ 9 6                          ◇ A 7 4 2
        ♣ 9 3               S          ♣ Q J 5

                        ♠ 9
                        ♡ A K 10 9 6 2
                        ◇ Q 8 5
                        ♣ A 7 4
```

WEST	NORTH	EAST	SOUTH
–	–	–	1♡
1♠	Dble (1)	3♠	4♡
End			

(1) Negative (take-out) double

West plays two top spades, forcing you to ruff. Let's see what happens if you continue with the ace and king of trumps at this stage. You will then be in trouble. You have two cards to knock out (♡Q and ◇A). If you play ♡10 next, West will win and force the South hand again with a spade. You can draw West's last trump but will then be out of trumps. You will have no protection against further spades when you knock out the diamond ace. You will fare no better if you play on diamonds before reverting to trumps. East will hold up his ace for one round, then give his partner a diamond ruff.

How should the hand be played? You can afford a trump loser and should surrender this trick at a time when the defenders can do no damage. In this case, the potential damage they can inflict is to force the South hand. Let's try ducking the *first* round of trumps, playing low towards dummy's jack. That's better. West is welcome to win with the queen because he cannot then force the South hand (a spade continuation will be ruffed in dummy). After winning West's return, you will draw trumps, set up the diamonds, and claim the contract. West does no better if he refuses to win the trump queen. You will draw two more rounds of trumps and – with two trumps remaining to West's one – establish the diamond suit.

Should I finesse in the trump suit?

You have a potential queen finesse in the trump suit. Should you take it? The answer will often depend on a grander view of the hand. Declarer played carelessly on this deal:

```
North–South game        ♠ A 7 2
Dealer South            ♡ A 5
                        ◇ K J 4 3
                        ♣ Q 8 7 2

      ♠ K Q J 9 6    N          ♠ 10 8 4 3
      ♡ Q 9 7 2             E   ♡ 6 3
      ◇ 9 6       W             ◇ 10 8 2
      ♣ A 5          S          ♣ 10 9 6 4

                        ♠ 5
                        ♡ K J 10 8 4
                        ◇ A Q 7 5
                        ♣ K J 3
```

WEST	NORTH	EAST	SOUTH
–	–	–	1♡
1♠	Dble (1)	Pass	2◇
Pass	2♠	Pass	3♣
Pass	3♡	Pass	4♡
End			

(1) Negative (take-out) double

Declarer won the spade lead, then played ace and another trump, finessing the jack. West won with the queen and played another spade, reducing declarer to two trumps – the same number as himself. The contract could no longer be made. If declarer drew West's trumps he would have no protection against the defenders' spades when the ace of clubs was knocked out. Nor would he fare any better by playing on clubs first. West would win and force declarer again in spades, leaving him with one trump to West's two.

What went wrong? Declarer could afford to lose two trump tricks and the ace of clubs. He should have maintained trump control by cashing the ace and king of trumps, then playing on clubs. West would be welcome to win and return a spade. After ruffing, declarer would simply play his winners in the minor suits, allowing the defenders to score two trump tricks. Game would then be made.

How would you have played the trump suit here?

Game all
Dealer South

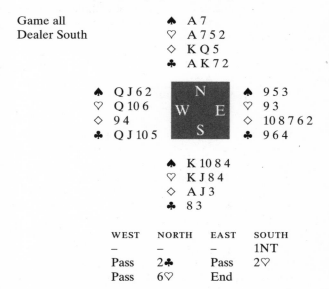

```
                    ♠ A 7
                    ♡ A 7 5 2
                    ◇ K Q 5
                    ♣ A K 7 2

    ♠ Q J 6 2          N          ♠ 9 5 3
    ♡ Q 10 6       W       E      ♡ 9 3
    ◇ 9 4              S          ◇ 10 8 7 6 2
    ♣ Q J 10 5                    ♣ 9 6 4

                    ♠ K 10 8 4
                    ♡ K J 8 4
                    ◇ A J 3
                    ♣ 8 3
```

WEST	NORTH	EAST	SOUTH
–	–	–	1NT
Pass	2♣	Pass	2♡
Pass	6♡	End	

You reach a respectable 6♡ and West leads the club queen, won with the king. Looking at the trump suit in isolation, you might decide to cash the ace of trumps and finesse the jack. One down! West will win with the queen and return another trump. Turn as you may, you will be one trick short.

You have seven side-suit winners and can bump this total to the required twelve tricks by drawing two rounds of trumps with the ace and king, then taking two black-suit ruffs in each hand. West may choose his moment to score the queen of trumps.

By spurning the trump finesse, you rescue the slam when trumps break 3-2 and West holds the queen. It's true that you give up most of your prospects when East holds ♡Q 10 9 3, but this lie of the cards is much less likely.

In contrast to the previous hand, it is sometimes right to finesse against the queen even when there are only four trumps out. How would you have handled the trumps on this deal:

Love all
Dealer South

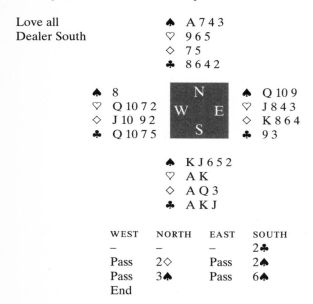

	♠ A 7 4 3
	♡ 9 6 5
	◇ 7 5
	♣ 8 6 4 2

♠ 8		♠ Q 10 9
♡ Q 10 7 2		♡ J 8 4 3
◇ J 10 9 2		◇ K 8 6 4
♣ Q 10 7 5		♣ 9 3

	♠ K J 6 5 2
	♡ A K
	◇ A Q 3
	♣ A K J

WEST	NORTH	EAST	SOUTH
–	–	–	2♣
Pass	2◇	Pass	2♠
Pass	3♠	Pass	6♠
End			

West leads ◇J and you win with the queen. If your next move is to cash the top two trumps, you will go down. You have a trump trick to lose and the club finesse is wrong. Instead you should cash the top two hearts and the ace of diamonds. You then ruff a diamond in dummy and ruff a heart in hand. With both red suits eliminated, you cross to the ace of trumps and play a second trump, finessing the jack. As it happens, the finesse wins and you have twelve tricks. If the finesse had lost to a doubleton queen, however, West would have been endplayed, forced to lead into your club tenace or to concede a ruff-and-discard.

Look back at the last two hands. On the first hand, a trump finesse was dangerous because if it lost West might play a third round of trumps. On the second hand, the trump finesse was safe: if it lost, West would be endplayed.

Finally, there is a class of hand where you play the trumps in such a way that if you do misguess, you will be able to end-play the defender who is left with a master trump.

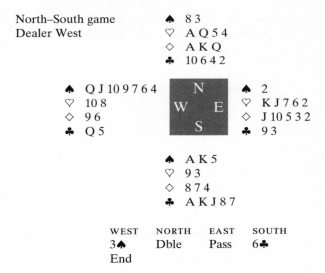

North–South game
Dealer West

North:
♠ 8 3
♡ A Q 5 4
♢ A K Q
♣ 10 6 4 2

West:
♠ Q J 10 9 7 6 4
♡ 10 8
♢ 9 6
♣ Q 5

East:
♠ 2
♡ K J 7 6 2
♢ J 10 5 3 2
♣ 9 3

South:
♠ A K 5
♡ 9 3
♢ 8 7 4
♣ A K J 8 7

WEST	NORTH	EAST	SOUTH
3♠	Dble	Pass	6♣
End			

Wasting no time in the auction, you arrive in Six Clubs. West leads ♠Q and you win with the ace. Both defenders follow to the ace of trumps. What now?

With West likely to hold seven spades to his partner's one, the chances are high that East started with three trumps to the queen. Nevertheless, it would be wrong to cross to dummy and take a trump finesse. If the finesse loses, you will go down when (as is likely) East holds the king of hearts.

Instead you should cash a second high trump. Here, the reward is instant. West's queen falls and you have twelve tricks. Suppose that West had shown out on the second round, leaving East with the bare queen of trumps. You would still make the slam! You would cash dummy's three diamond winners, then play a spade towards the king, just in case East holds another spade. You would then exit with a trump to East's queen, forcing him lead into dummy's ♡A Q or to concede a ruff-and-discard.

POINTS TO REMEMBER

1. The decision whether to draw trumps (and, if so, how many rounds) is more complicated than many players admit. These are the most frequent reasons for declining to play on the trump suit immediately:

- You need to ruff some losers in the short-trump hand
- You need to take a quick discard, perhaps of a loser exposed by the opening lead
- You need to establish a quick discard before your last stopper in a suit is removed
- You will need one of dummy's trumps as an entry to the long cards in a suit you plan to establish.

2. By drawing only some of the outstanding trumps (for example, drawing two rounds when there are five trumps out), you may aid your ruffing prospects. You will be able to ruff the fourth round of a side suit such as K Q x x opposite A x x when the defender short in this suit does not hold the missing trump.

3. When you will have to lose a trump trick, or can afford to do so if trumps break badly, choose the right moment to surrender it. Do so when the opponents will have the least chance to cause any damage.

4. When deciding whether to finesse against the queen of trumps, consider what may happen if the finesse loses. If the defender on lead will be able to make a damaging play (for example, drawing a further round of trumps), consider whether you will be better off by not taking the finesse.

TEST YOURSELF

♠ Q J 10 6
♡ Q 7
◇ A 6 5

A.

♣ K J 9 2

◇J led

West leads ◇J
against 4♠. How
will you play the
contract?

♠ A 9 5 4 2
♡ K 9 3
◇ K 9 2
♣ Q 8

B.

♠ 8 4
♡ A Q J 10 6
◇ A J 9 6 2
♣ 5

♣K led

West leads ♣K.
How would you
play (a) 7♠, (b)
6♠?

♠ A K Q 9 7 2
♡ K 9
◇ –
♣ A 10 9 7 2

C.

♠ K 10 8 6
♡ 8 5 4
◇ A K J 9
♣ A 6

♣Q led

West leads ♣Q
against 4♠. How
will you play the
contract?

♠ A J 5 4 2
♡ K 9 3
◇ Q 8 4
♣ K 7

ANSWERS

A. If you win the diamond lead in dummy and take a trump finesse, which loses, you will be in trouble. West will persist with diamonds and you will have a loser in every suit. A better plan is to win the diamond lead in your hand and play ♣Q, continuing with another club if the first round is ducked. You will then be able to discard your diamond loser on the established club winner. All in good time, you will draw trumps.

B. In the grand slam, you will need trumps to break 3-2. You should draw trumps straight away, complaining loudly about your bad luck if trumps prove to be 4-1. In a small slam you can afford to lose a trump trick. At trick two you should lead a small trump from your hand. Dummy still has a trump, to guard against a club continuation. You will win the return, draw trumps, then run dummy's heart suit. If instead you play trumps from the top, you are likely to go down whenever the trumps break 4-1.

C. If East ever gains the lead, he may put the contract at risk by leading a heart through your king. You should therefore play the trump suit in such a way that East cannot gain the lead. Win the club lead with the king, cross to the king of trumps, and lead a second round of trumps. If East follows low, finesse the jack. You can afford to lose a doubleton queen with West, because you will subsequently throw one of your hearts on dummy's diamonds. If instead you rise with the ace of trumps, West showing out, East may ruff an early diamond with the trump queen and send a heart through your king.

3. Battling for the Part-Score

What is the biggest difference between bidding at social rubber bridge and the auctions in a tournament game? There is little doubt about it. It is the intensity of the battle on part-score deals. At social bridge the thinking may be: That's a relief, they've stopped in Two Diamonds. In the tournament game, players are always reluctant to let the opponents win the auction at such a modest level. The very fact that they have stopped so low suggests that the points are evenly distributed between the two sides. Why let the enemy choose trumps?

In this chapter we will look in turn at the main situations where you should contest boldly for the part-score.

The opponents stop low in a trump fit

You are sitting North and the bidding begins like this:

WEST	NORTH	· EAST	SOUTH
1♡	Pass	2♡	Pass
Pass	?		

What deductions can you make? The responder will hold around 6–9 high-card points. The opener, who has made no move towards game, probably holds about 11–15 points. Don't say to yourself: 'If they're both maximum, they may have game on. I'd better not give them another chance.' Say instead: 'The points are evenly divided between the two sides, near enough. Perhaps we can make a contract or push them to the three-level.'

It's not just a matter of points, either. When one side has a trump fit, so will the other. Why is that? On the above auction North–South may well have a 5–4 trump fit. That is 9 hearts between them and only 17 non-hearts. You and your partner therefore hold 22 non-hearts between you. You will have an 8-card fit somewhere even if the cards are distributed 8-7-7 between the remaining three suits. Often you will have a 9-card fit. With a near-guaranteed fit somewhere, and around half the points in the pack, you must get into the auction!

Bidding in the pass-out seat is known as 'protection'. The defender who contests the auction may be relatively light, in terms of high-card points. The mere fact that the opponents have stopped low entitles him to place his partner with some values.

Let's look at a typical deal:

Love all
Dealer West

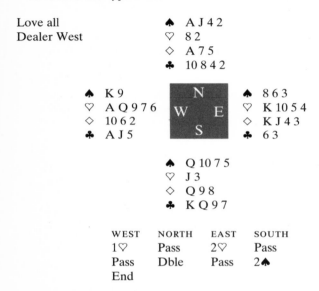

	♠ A J 4 2	
	♡ 8 2	
	◇ A 7 5	
	♣ 10 8 4 2	

♠ K 9	♠ 8 6 3
♡ A Q 9 7 6	♡ K 10 5 4
◇ 10 6 2	◇ K J 4 3
♣ A J 5	♣ 6 3

	♠ Q 10 7 5	
	♡ J 3	
	◇ Q 9 8	
	♣ K Q 9 7	

WEST	NORTH	EAST	SOUTH
1♡	Pass	2♡	Pass
Pass	Dble	Pass	2♠
End			

The opponents find a heart fit and stop at the two-level. North was not strong enough to double on the first round but, in the pass-out seat, he does contest the auction. The 4-4 spade fit comes to light and East–West now have two options. They can let this contract stand (with two out of three finesses right, eight tricks will be made). Or they can advance to 3♡, which will go one down.

You may be thinking: all very well when there is a spade fit and the finesses are working! We have already seen, however, that when the opponents have a trump fit the odds are high that you will have one too. As for whether the cards lie favourably or not, it is strange but true that this does not matter very much. If the cards lie poorly for North–South and 2♠ goes down, the cards will lie correspondingly well for East–West and they would have done well in their heart contract.

Sometimes you can tell that the opponents have a trump fit, even though their bidding has not admitted this explicitly. What do you make of this auction:

WEST	NORTH	EAST	SOUTH
–	–	–	1♣
Pass	1NT	Pass	2♣
?			

Since North declined to bid a 4-card suit over 1♣, he will hold at least three clubs and nearly always four. The odds are high that North–South have a 9-card club fit and it will rarely be right for East–West to allow this contract to play. One or other defender should contest, usually with a take-out double. At the very least, it should be possible to push the opponents to 3♣.

The situation would be much the same after an opposing auction of 1◇ – 1NT – 2◇, although it is possible here that responder is long in clubs.

The opponents stop low after preference

The outlook for protection is nowhere near so promising when responder has merely given preference, rather than a direct raise:

WEST	NORTH	EAST	SOUTH
–	1◇	Pass	1♠
Pass	2♣	Pass	2◇
Pass	Pass	?	

They have stopped low, yes, but they may not have a primary trump fit. Very often the diamond fit will be only 5-2, which does not guarantee you an 8-card fit your way. Another discouraging factor is that three of the suits have already been bid. Nevertheless, you should consider action on hands of this type:

(1) ♠ A 10 8
   ♡ K Q 10 2
   ◇ 10 7 4 3
   ♣ A 9

(2) ♠ K 8
   ♡ 10 8 7 6 4 2
   ◇ 9 8
   ♣ A 10 2

On hand (1) you will double, hoping to find a resting place in hearts or, despite South's response, in spades. On hand (2) your heart suit did not justify an overcall on the first round. Now, with 10 points or so marked in your partner's hand, you will contest with 2♡.

The opener rebids his suit

Many players fail to realise that protection is an option on auctions of this type.

WEST	West	North	East	South
♠ A Q 8 3	–	1♣	Pass	1♠
♡ J 8 5	Pass	2♣	Pass	Pass
◇ A 10 9 5	?			
♣ 6 4				

The odds favour re-opening with a take-out double now. When partner has something good in clubs sitting over the opener, he can pass out the double for penalties. Otherwise he will bid two of a red suit. You may end in a playable spot, or perhaps push the opponents one level higher.

WEST	West	North	East	South
♠ K 8 2	–	1♡	Pass	1♠
♡ 5	Pass	2♡	Pass	Pass
◇ K 10 9 5	?			
♣ A 9 8 5 2				

It is dangerous to contest the auction now, since you would have to play at the three-level. If you do decide to act on such a hand (perhaps non-vulnerable, at match-points), a double is more flexible than the Unusual 2NT. A double may gain handsomely when partner has a stack of hearts and can pass for penalties.

The opening bid is followed by two passes

You are sitting West and an opening bid on your left runs to you:

WEST	NORTH	EAST	SOUTH
–	1♡	Pass	Pass
?			

What is your normal reaction to this situation? You should be very reluctant to let the opponents choose trumps at such a low level. Whenever possible you should contest the auction, with an overcall or a take-out double. In general, you should be willing to bid with around 3 points less than you would need in the second seat.

Suppose you hold one of these hands:

(1)	♠ Q 10 8 3	(2)	♠ 6 2	(3)	♠ K 9 2
	♡ 10 4		♡ Q 9 7		♡ K J 4
	◇ A 9 7 2		◇ 10 3		◇ K 10 7 4
	♣ K 6 4		♣ A Q 9 7 6 3		♣ Q 8 3

Hand (1) is a minimum for a double in the protective seat. Add another king and you would have doubled in the second seat – that's the test. Hand (2) is well worth a protective 2♣ overcall. Such an overcall would have been unsound in the second seat, but in the protective seat you must stretch to keep the bidding alive. On hand (3) you can overcall 1NT, which shows only about 11–15 points in fourth position.

Since the minimum for all these actions is around 3 points less than you would need in the second seat, partner must show corresponding restraint with any response. Roughly speaking, he should deduct 3 points from his own hand before determining his response, if any.

Suppose the bidding starts:

WEST	NORTH	EAST	SOUTH
–	1♡	Pass	Pass
Dble	Pass	?	

What would you respond on these East hands:

(1)	♠ A Q 7 2	(2)	♠ Q 4	(3)	♠ A J 7 4
	♡ J 8 5		♡ A Q 7 2		♡ 10 8 7 2
	◇ 10 6 3		◇ K 9 6 3		◇ 4
	♣ Q 7 2		♣ Q 8 4		♣ A K 10 3

Hand (1) would be an easy 2♠ response (8–11 points) opposite a second-seat double. You should respond only 1♠, facing a protective double. On (2) you would respond 3NT to a second-seat double; now you will bid only 2NT. Hand (3) is worth a cue-bid response of 2♡ (see Chapter 1). If partner rebids 2♠ you will raise to only 3♠. Facing a second-seat double, you would not allow the bidding to stop short of game.

The situation is much the same when an opening pre-empt is followed by two passes:

WEST	NORTH	EAST	SOUTH
–	3◇	Pass	Pass
?			

Sitting West, you might hold one of these hands:

(1) ♠ A J 8 3	(2) ♠ 6 2	(3) ♠ A 5
♡ K 9 4 2	♡ A Q J 9 7	♡ 8 4
◇ 10 3	◇ 8 5	◇ K 10 7
♣ K 8 5	♣ A 10 7 2	♣ A Q J 8 4 3

Hand (1) would not justify a second-seat double. In the protective seat you are entitled to mentally add a king to your hand. With 14 points and two four-card majors, you would have a minimum double in second seat. So, go ahead and double. Partner should allow for the fact that you may hold no more than this.

It's the same with (2). To bid 3♡ in the second seat would be quite a gamble. In the protective seat, the odds swing in favour of the overcall. Remember that your partner might have passed with as many as 14 points, if his hand is balanced. You may have a game on.

With hand (3) you would try your luck in 3NT, hoping for a high card or two opposite.

When the decision to protect is borderline, you are perfectly entitled to take into account the reaction of the player on your right. Did he seem to contemplate a raise of the pre-empt? If so, he is more likely to hold the missing points than your partner.

Let's look at a quite different situation. What are your normal thoughts when you sit in the fourth seat here:

WEST	NORTH	EAST	SOUTH
–	1NT (1)	Pass	Pass
?			

(1) Weak no-trump, 12–14 points.

You are in the protective seat, yes, but South may hold anything up to a moderate 11-count. In general, you should hold the same values for any action in fourth seat (penalty double, or overcall) as you would in the second seat. This applies particularly when you are contemplating a close penalty double. Remember that you will not be on lead – partner may strike out in some undesired direction.

Protection by the opener (rubber bridge)

You open 1♠, say, and the auction continues like this:

WEST	NORTH	EAST	SOUTH
–	–	–	1♠
2◇	Pass	Pass	?

What should your general reaction be? To some extent, it depends on what a double of 2◇ by North would have meant. If you are playing penalty doubles of overcalls (normal at rubber bridge), North is unlikely to hold more than 8 points or so. Would you contest further on these South hands?

(1) ♠ A Q 8 7 2	(2) ♠ K Q 9 7 3	(3) ♠ A K 9 6 2
♡ K 3	♡ A Q 7 6 2	♡ K 10 9 4
◇ 8 7 5	◇ J 8	◇ 9
♣ A 9 6	♣ 2	♣ A 10 8

It would be a poor effort to rebid 2♠ on (1). If your partner held 6 points or so and three spades, he would have made the raise himself. You should pass.

On hand (2) you should contest with 2♡. You are quite likely to hold five hearts for this bid. On many hands with four hearts, such as (3), you would contest with a take-out double instead.

Protection by the opener (duplicate, with negative doubles)

In duplicate bridge it is normal to play doubles of overcalls for take-out. These are known as 'negative doubles'. When responder has length and strength in the overcaller's suit, he will often pass even when quite strong. He is relying on the opener to protect – preferably with a (take-out) double, which will then be passed for penalties.

When the opener is short in the overcaller's suit, he should re-open with a double, even on a minimum hand:

WEST	NORTH	EAST	SOUTH
–	–	–	1♡
2♣	Pass (1)	Pass	?

(1) A double would have been for take-out.

South should then double on all these hands:

(1) ♠ A J 8	(2) ♠ K 9 3	(3) ♠ A K 9 6
♡ K 10 9 7 6	♡ A Q 7 5 2	♡ A K 9 4 3
◇ A 10 6	◇ Q J 7 2	◇ 9
♣ 8 5	♣ 4	♣ A 10 5

On the first two hands, you rather expect partner to be strong in clubs. This prospect is enhanced by the fact that East did not raise the overcall. You double in the expectation that partner will choose to pass. On (3) you do not expect partner to be long in clubs. Nevertheless, your own strength justifies competing further. Once again, you should double for take-out. If partner responds 2◇, as is likely, you will correct to 2♡, offering a choice of the majors.

A fourth-seat overcall is followed by two passes

Some players are uncertain what to do here:

NORTH	West	North	East	South
♠ 10 5	–	–	–	1♡
♡ J 4	Pass	2♣	2♠	Pass
◇ K J 7 4	Pass	?		
♣ A Q 9 6 2				

North should contest the auction with a double, for take-out. This is a much more sensible treatment than playing a double for penalties. It is rarely profitable to make a penalty double when your trumps lie under declarer.

The opponents stop low after partner has opened

When your partner has shown values by opening the bidding, you should be particularly reluctant to let the opponents choose trumps at a low level. Suppose you are East here:

WEST	NORTH	EAST	SOUTH
1♦	Dble	Pass	1♡
Pass	Pass	?	

The opponents have no right to choose trumps and play at the one-level! Even when you are quite weak, you should contest the part-score. You know, from the lack of enterprise shown by the other side, that partner must have a respectable hand.

Each of these East hands justifies further action:

(1)	♠ J 9 8 2	(2)	♠ Q 10 7 6 2	(3)	♠ 10 3
	♡ 10 5		♡ 7 4		♡ 9 7 6 4
	♦ J 10 6		♦ 9 5		♦ Q 10 4
	♣ Q 8 7 4		♣ J 9 6 2		♣ Q 9 6 5

On (1) you would double for take-out. On (2) you would bid 1♠. With hand (3) you would contest with 2♦. In each case partner will know you are weak because you did not bid on the first round. Contesting the part-score on such hands is much safer than it looks. What you can't afford to do is to sit back and allow the opponents an easy ride in their one-level contract.

SUMMARY

(1) When in the pass-out seat, always give some thought before letting the opponents play at a low level. The points are probably equally divided between the sides and there is no reason why the opponents should be allowed to choose trumps.

(2) Be particularly vigorous with your competition when the opponents have found a trump fit, then stopped at a low level. If they have a fit, your side will have a fit somewhere too.

(3) In many protective situations, the most flexible competitive action is a take-out double. Lean towards this action when partner may be

strong in the opponents' suit and did not have a penalty double available to him.

TEST YOURSELF

A. You are East and the bidding begins like this:

WEST	NORTH	EAST	SOUTH
–	1◇	Pass	2◇
Pass	Pass	?	

What would you say, if anything, on these hands:

	(1)	♠ A J 9 4	(2)	♠ K J 8 3 2	(3)	♠ 8
		♡ K J 4 2		♡ 8 3		♡ K Q J 9
		◇ 9 3 2		◇ 10 5		◇ A 9 7 3
		♣ 8 6		♣ K J 7 2		♣ J 10 7 2

B. You are West and the auction starts:

WEST	NORTH	EAST	SOUTH
–	1♡	Pass	Pass
?			

Would you protect on these West hands? If so, what would you bid?

	(1)	♠ A 9 4	(2)	♠ A K 10 8	(3)	♠ A 8
		♡ J 5		♡ 10 8 6 3		♡ K 10 8 2
		◇ K 10 3 2		◇ 4		◇ K J 7
		♣ Q 9 6 5		♣ K J 7 2		♣ Q 10 4 2

C. You are East and the bidding begins like this:

WEST	NORTH	EAST	SOUTH
1◇	Pass	1♠	2♡
Pass	Pass	?	

What would you say on these hands:

(1) ♠ A 10 8 3
    ♡ K 10 4 2
    ◇ K 3
    ♣ J 8 5

(2) ♠ K 10 8 7 2
    ♡ 8 3
    ◇ Q 5
    ♣ A Q 7 2

(3) ♠ A 9 8 4 2
    ♡ K Q 8 2
    ◇ 10 7
    ♣ 6 3

ANSWERS

A. The opponents have a fit, but stopped at a low level. You should be very reluctant to pass out 2◇. On (1) you are happy to double for take-out. With (2) you bid 2♠. You can hardly double on (3), with only one spade. Bid 2♡. Partner will be short in diamonds and is likely to hold some heart support.

B. On (1) you should protect with a take-out double. Partner will be conservative with his response, realising that you may be light in the protective seat. Hand (2) is not suitable for a double because of the diamond singleton; overcall 1♠ instead. Hand (3) is fine for a protective 1NT, showing 11–15 points.

C. Hand (1) contains 11 points and a sound stopper in hearts. You should bid 2NT, inviting a game in no-trumps. Your side has the balance of the points on (2) and you should double, for take-out. You are not quite strong enough for 3♣, which would often carry the bidding too high. With (3) you would pass. Remember that a double would be for take-out, not penalties. Nor would a penalty double be attractive here, with your trumps lying under the declarer.

4. Count Signals

Suppose you sat down to play bridge with a complete stranger, without any discussion beforehand. What type of signals would you expect him to play? The best bet would be: attitude signals (high spot-card is encouraging) on your suits, and count signals (high spot-card shows an even number of cards) on declarer's suits.

As the years pass by, more and more players prefer to use count signals throughout. By the time six or seven tricks have been played, they will have a complete count on the hand – with great benefit to their defence.

Count signals on declarer's suits

We will look first at the basics of playing count signals on declarer's suits, then move to the possibly new area of playing count signals on your own suits. This type of hand may be familiar:

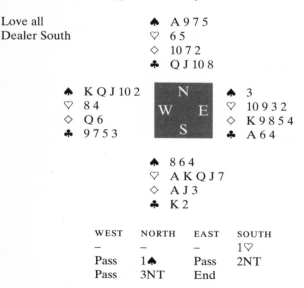

Love all
Dealer South

	♠	A 9 7 5
	♡	6 5
	◇	10 7 2
	♣	Q J 10 8

♠ K Q J 10 2		♠ 3
♡ 8 4	N	♡ 10 9 3 2
◇ Q 6	W E	◇ K 9 8 5 4
♣ 9 7 5 3	S	♣ A 6 4

	♠	8 6 4
	♡	A K Q J 7
	◇	A J 3
	♣	K 2

WEST	NORTH	EAST	SOUTH
–	–	–	1♡
Pass	1♠	Pass	2NT
Pass	3NT	End	

West attacks in spades and declarer wins the third round with the ace. He plays a club to the king and a club back to dummy's queen. Suppose you are sitting East. Should you win this trick or not?

If declarer holds three clubs you must hold up the ace for one more round, cutting him off from dummy's fourth club. Suppose the cards lie as in the diagram, however. Now it would be fatal to hold up the ace a second time. With a second club trick in the bag, declarer would claim the contract.

To decide when to take your ace, you need to know how many clubs declarer has. Only West can provide this information, and he does this by declaring his own length in the suit. Here West would signal with the 7 on the first round of clubs, the 3 on the second round. You will now know that West has either four clubs or two. If he has four, you should win the ace of clubs on the second round. If he has two, it will make no difference when you take the ace. You duly win the second round of clubs and make a safe switch to hearts, putting the contract one down.

Count signals can prove just as useful against suit contracts.

Love all
Dealer South

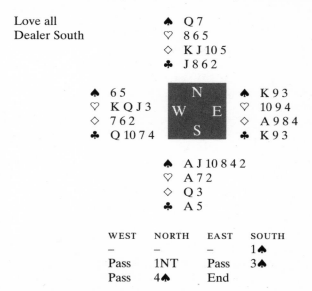

```
                       ♠  Q 7
                       ♡  8 6 5
                       ◇  K J 10 5
                       ♣  J 8 6 2

   ♠  6 5                          ♠  K 9 3
   ♡  K Q J 3          N           ♡  10 9 4
   ◇  7 6 2         W     E        ◇  A 9 8 4
   ♣  Q 10 7 4         S           ♣  K 9 3

                       ♠  A J 10 8 4 2
                       ♡  A 7 2
                       ◇  Q 3
                       ♣  A 5
```

WEST	NORTH	EAST	SOUTH
–	–	–	1♠
Pass	1NT	Pass	3♠
Pass	4♠	End	

Take the East cards again. The opponents overbid to a poor spade game and your partner leads ♡K. Declarer allows this card to hold and wins heart continuation. He next plays the queen of diamonds, overtaking with dummy's king. What should you do?

The answer is that you should have a close look at the spot-card played by your partner to this trick. In this case it is the 2, showing three diamonds and leaving declarer with two. If you make the mistake of winning the first round of diamonds, declarer will later be able to throw a club on dummy's diamonds. Game made.

Suppose instead that you allow dummy's king of diamonds to win. Declarer will pick up your king of trumps but he will have no way to avoid three further losers in the side suits. That will be one down.

If South's ◇Q had been a singleton, your partner would have signalled with ◇6 (second highest from 7 6 3 2, see the next section), suggesting four cards in the suit. You would then have won the first diamond trick. Not only would declarer score no diamond tricks at all, he would be unable to take the trump finesse!

Sometimes partner's count signal in one of declarer's suits will allow you to determine how many tricks declarer has.

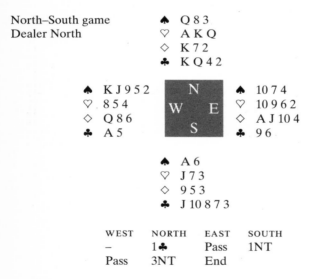

North–South game	♠ Q 8 3
Dealer North	♡ A K Q
	◇ K 7 2
	♣ K Q 4 2

♠ K J 9 5 2
♡ 8 5 4
◇ Q 8 6
♣ A 5

♠ 10 7 4
♡ 10 9 6 2
◇ A J 10 4
♣ 9 6

♠ A 6
♡ J 7 3
◇ 9 5 3
♣ J 10 8 7 3

WEST	NORTH	EAST	SOUTH
–	1♣	Pass	1NT
Pass	3NT	End	

Sitting West, you lead ♠5 against 3NT. Dummy's queen wins the trick and partner plays the 4, suggesting three spades. Declarer continues with ♣K, your partner contributing the 9. You allow the king to win and capture the next round of clubs, partner playing the 6. We will discuss in a moment how you can tell whether partner has two or four cards when he plays high-low. Here South declined to bid a suit at the one-level and is therefore more likely to hold 2-3-3-5 shape than 2-4-4-3.

How many top tricks can you count for declarer in that case? He has four clubs, three hearts and two spades. That is nine, already! Unless you can quickly cash four diamond tricks the game will be made. Taking your only chance, you switch to the queen of diamonds – with gratifying results.

Does partner have four cards or two?

Once you know whether partner has an even or odd number of cards in a suit, you can often tell from bidding (or the play so far) exactly how many cards he holds. The occasional ambiguity between four and two cards can usually be resolved by signalling with the second-best card followed by the fourth-best, when you hold four cards.

Look at this hand from West's viewpoint:

North–South game
Dealer South

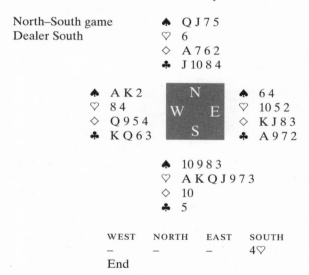

```
                    ♠ Q J 7 5
                    ♡ 6
                    ♢ A 7 6 2
                    ♣ J 10 8 4

    ♠ A K 2            N            ♠ 6 4
    ♡ 8 4                           ♡ 10 5 2
    ♢ Q 9 5 4     W        E        ♢ K J 8 3
    ♣ K Q 6 3          S            ♣ A 9 7 2

                    ♠ 10 9 8 3
                    ♡ A K Q J 9 7 3
                    ♢ 10
                    ♣ 5
```

WEST	NORTH	EAST	SOUTH
–	–	–	4♡
End			

West leads the ace of spades, drawing the 6 and the 3 from the closed hands. Since dummy has the queen and jack of the suit, and West would scarcely lead the ace of spades unless it was backed by the king, East's 6 will be a count signal.

West continues with the king of spades and this time sees the 4 and the 10 appear from the closed hands. A spade continuation will beat the contract, as you see. But with East showing an even number of cards, and South playing a deceptive 10 from his hand, West may fear that East holds four spades rather than two. Suppose that East did start with ♠9 8 6 4, however. Playing the recommended method, he would signal with the 8 (second best) followed by the 4 (fourth best). His actual 6 and 4 must therefore be from a doubleton. West trustfully plays a third spade and the game goes one down.

Even if declarer is clever with his own play of the pips, the 'second then fourth' method will usually allow you to determine whether partner holds four cards or two.

Do not signal with a valuable card

When signalling you should not, of course, waste a card that may be needed for trick-taking purposes. We have just seen that you would signal with a second-best 8 from 9 8 5 4. If instead you were giving a count signal from Q J 5 2 or J 10 5 2, you would retain your honours and play the 5.

Similarly, there will be many occasions where you cannot afford to play high from a doubleton:

$$\heartsuit \quad K\,9\,6\,3$$
$$\heartsuit \quad Q\,J\,8\,5 \qquad\qquad \heartsuit \quad 10\,2$$
$$\heartsuit \quad A\,7\,4$$

When South leads the ace it would be foolish for East to give count by playing the 10. Declarer would then score three tricks in the suit.

You think this is so obvious that I should not have mentioned it? Playing in an international trial, one of Britain's top bridge names, veteran of two Bermuda bowls, allowed my partner to make an impossible grand slam with such a signal!

Don't save declarer a guess

Some players thoughtlessly give a count signal, even when declarer has a critical guess in the suit. Suppose South has to tackle this diamond combination:

$\diamond$ K Q 10 3

$\diamond$ J 9 4 2 $\diamond$ 8 7

$\diamond$ A 6 5

Declarer leads $\diamond$5 from hand. If West 'does what comes naturally' and signals with the 4, he may regret it. Declarer will win with the king, and return to the ace. When West's 2 appears (either on the second round, or the third round), declarer may read him for four diamonds and take a successful finesse of dummy's 10.

'But I might have been fooling him,' West may say. For every defender who will attempt to fool you by giving a false signal, there will be five defenders willing to assist you by giving a true signal. As declarer, you should cash in on those odds, believing the signals that are given.

Count signals on your own suits

We will see in Chapter 9 how it is possible to combine two types of signalling (attitude and count) in response to the opening lead of an honour. For the moment, we will look at the general advantages that may be gained by playing count signals, rather than attitude signals, when you or your partner lead to a trick.

West was glad to be playing count signals on this hand:

East–West game   ♠ A K 7 3

Dealer South   ♡ J 9 4

                  $\diamond$ 10 9 7

                  ♣ Q J 7

♠ 10 6		♠ J 8 5 2
♡ 8 7 3	N	♡ K 10 5 2
$\diamond$ A Q 4	W E	$\diamond$ 8 3
♣ K 10 8 4 3	S	♣ 9 6 2

                  ♠ Q 9 4

                  ♡ A Q 6

                  $\diamond$ K J 6 5 2

                  ♣ A 5

WEST	NORTH	EAST	SOUTH
–	–	–	1$\diamond$
Pass	1♠	Pass	1NT
Pass	3NT	End	

West led ♣4 against 3NT and dummy's queen won the trick. East's count signal of the 2 showed that he held either three clubs or one. Declarer now ran ◇10, East signalling with the 8. Do you see how quickly West is able to build up a picture of the whole hand? East's ◇8 suggested a doubleton, leaving South with five diamonds. It was already a sound bet that South's shape was either 3-3-5-2 or 2-4-5-2.

Expecting South's ace of clubs to be bare now, West played another club. This did indeed drive out the ace and when declarer continued with diamonds West was able to cash three club tricks, putting the contract one down.

Let's change that last deal slightly:

East–West game   ♠ A K 7 3
Dealer South   ♡ J 9 4
                    ◇ 10 9 7
                    ♣ Q J 7

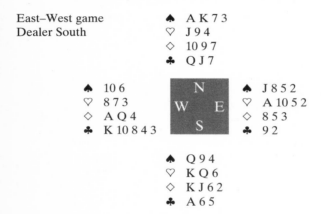

  ♠ 10 6   ♠ J 8 5 2
  ♡ 8 7 3   ♡ A 10 5 2
  ◇ A Q 4   ◇ 8 5 3
  ♣ K 10 8 4 3   ♣ 9 2

          ♠ Q 9 4
          ♡ K Q 6
          ◇ K J 6 2
          ♣ A 6 5

The bidding and the contract (3NT) are still the same. West's club lead is won with the queen, but this time East signals with the 9 to show an even number of cards in the suit. When West takes the diamond queen he knows that a club return cannot force out the ace. Indeed, it will give declarer a third club trick. Needing to reach his partner's hand, West switches to ♡8. East wins with the ace and leads a club from his side of the table. The club suit is cleared and West will put the contract two down when he comes on lead with the diamond ace.

As you see, count signals allow you to beat the contract in both cases. Without such assistance, West would have to guess what to do. 'Guess' is a word that makes good players wince. They like to *know* what to do!

Count signals work well on many other holdings:

```
               ♣  J 10 6 3
   ♣  K Q 8 4              ♣  9 7 2
               ♣  A 5
```

Defending a no-trump contract, you lead ♣4, not overjoyed to see dummy's jack win the trick. Partner's count signal of the 2 is better news, however. It shows an odd number of clubs, leaving declarer with either two clubs or four. Much of the time you will know from the bidding that South cannot hold four clubs. In any case, a low club continuation when you regain the lead will probably be the best chance of beating the contract.

Here, the message from partner's signal is less favourable:

```
               ♣  J 10 6 3
   ♣  K Q 8 4              ♣  9 2
               ♣  A 7 5
```

Once again you lead ♣4 against a no-trump contract, dummy's jack winning the trick. Partner's 9 warns you that you should not continue clubs when you gain the lead.

Even if your general preference is to play attitude signals on your own leads, it still makes good sense to signal count when you cannot beat dummy's card. An attitude signal would be pointless in a situation like this:

```
               ♣  K 10
   ♣  J 8 6 2              ♣  9 7 3
               ♣  A Q 5 4
```

West leads ♣2 against a no-trump contract and dummy's 10 wins the trick. East's 3 tells his partner that declarer has four clubs and that any further attack on this suit will be unproductive. If East instead held ♣9 7 5 3, he would signal with the 7 (second best from four). This would mark declarer with three clubs, perhaps making it worthwhile for the defenders to persevere with the suit.

The same principle applies when your attitude to partner's lead will be clear by the time the trick has been completed:

♡　K 10 4

♡　Q J 9 3　　　　　　　♡　8 7 6 2

♡　A 5

Partner leads an unlucky ♡Q, declarer playing low from the dummy. Declarer is about to win the trick with the ace and a discouraging attitude signal would be superfluous. You should play the 7, giving partner a count on the suit.

On the next deal, a count signal at trick 1 guided West in his defence against a slam.

East–West game　　　　　　♠　J 10 8 3
Dealer South　　　　　　　♡　A 6
　　　　　　　　　　　　　◇　10
　　　　　　　　　　　　　♣　A K J 10 8 6

```
        ♠  K 4        N        ♠  7
        ♡  K Q 7 5 3           ♡  J 10 9 4 2
        ◇  J 8 5 2   W   E     ◇  A 9 6 4 3
        ♣  9 4        S        ♣  7 2
```

　　　　　　　　　　　　　♠　A Q 9 6 5 2
　　　　　　　　　　　　　♡　8
　　　　　　　　　　　　　◇　K Q 7
　　　　　　　　　　　　　♣　Q 5 3

WEST	NORTH	EAST	SOUTH
–	–	–	1♠
Pass	3♣	Pass	3♠
Pass	4♠	Pass	4NT
Pass	5♡	Pass	6♠
End			

West led ♡K against Six Spades, dummy's ace winning the trick. East duly followed with the 2, to indicate an odd number of hearts. Declarer ran the jack of trumps to West's king and the key moment of the hand had been reached. What should West play next? Had East signalled an even number of hearts, West would know that the heart queen would stand up. East's actual signal of the 2 (backed up by South's willingness to use Blackwood despite holding no high-card control in the heart suit) strongly suggested that declarer held no more hearts. West switched bravely to a diamond and the slam was one down.

Count signals to expose declarer's deception

Resourceful declarers tend to false-card freely, in an attempt to
disguise their holding in a suit. Such deception can often be exposed
by a count signal. Look at this deal:

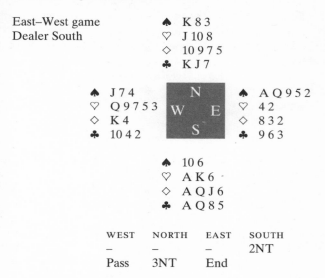

East–West game ♠ K 8 3
Dealer South ♡ J 10 8
◇ 10 9 7 5
♣ K J 7

♠ J 7 4 ♠ A Q 9 5 2
♡ Q 9 7 5 3 ♡ 4 2
◇ K 4 ◇ 8 3 2
♣ 10 4 2 ♣ 9 6 3

♠ 10 6
♡ A K 6
◇ A Q J 6
♣ A Q 8 5

WEST	NORTH	EAST	SOUTH
–	–	–	2NT
Pass	3NT	End	

Sitting West, you lead ♡5 against 3NT, drawing the 8, 4 and king.
(Worried about the spade situation, declarer is doing his best to look
like a man holding ♡A K doubleton.) He crosses to the king of clubs
and runs ◇10 to your king. What should you do next?

Many defenders would fall for the deception, continuing with
another heart on the assumption that declarer's ace is now bare. If
you play count signals, you will know that this is not the case. East
would not have played the 4 from ♡6 4 2. Declarer must therefore
have at least one small spot-card alongside his ace and a heart
continuation cannot succeed. What chance is there, then?

There is little point in crossing to partner's hand for a heart
switch. You know that he started with at most two hearts and you will have no
entry for the long hearts. The only remaining chance is that you can
take four (or more) tricks in the spade suit. You therefore switch to
♠J, causing partner's eyes to light up. Two down!

West tumbled into declarer's trap on the next deal. Would you have side-stepped round it?

North–South game
Dealer South

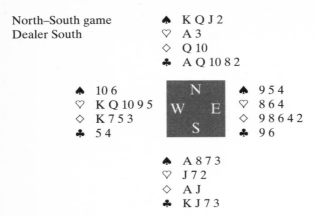

```
                    ♠ K Q J 2
                    ♡ A 3
                    ♢ Q 10
                    ♣ A Q 10 8 2

  ♠ 10 6                          ♠ 9 5 4
  ♡ K Q 10 9 5        N           ♡ 8 6 4
  ♢ K 7 5 3        W     E        ♢ 9 8 6 4 2
  ♣ 5 4               S           ♣ 9 6

                    ♠ A 8 7 3
                    ♡ J 7 2
                    ♢ A J
                    ♣ K J 7 3
```

A small slam in spades was the best contract since the diamond loser can be thrown on the fifth club. South arrived in Six Clubs instead. He won the king of hearts lead with dummy's ace and drew trumps in two rounds. After cashing three rounds of spades, removing that suit from the scene, he led the jack of hearts to West's queen. By leading the jack he hoped to create the impression that this was his last heart. Suppose you had been West. What would you have done next?

Fearing that declarer had no more hearts, West was reluctant to concede a ruff-and-discard by playing a third round of the suit. He switched to a low diamond, hoping that East held the jack and declarer would misguess. Not the best! Declarer now had twelve tricks.

Such a deception is easily unmasked by a count signal from East at trick 1. The 4 followed by the 6 would show three hearts, leaving declarer with three. West would then know that it was safe to exit with a third round of hearts. Forced back onto the diamond finesse, declarer would go one down.

POINTS TO REMEMBER

1. There is little benefit in playing attitude signals on declarer's suits. Count signals are universally played. A high card shows an even number of cards in the suit, a low card shows an odd number.

2. When partner leads a suit, and you don't have to play a high card in an attempt to win the trick, you have a choice of two methods: attitude signals, or count signals. An increasing number of players prefer to play count signals.

3. Even if your general preference is to give attitude signals on partner's leads, you should give a count signal when your attitude will be obvious by the time the trick is over.

4. When signalling from four small, play the second-best card followed by the fourth-best. This will usually allow partner to distinguish between four cards and two.

TEST YOURSELF

A.

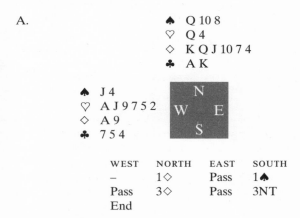

```
                    ♠  Q 10 8
                    ♡  Q 4
                    ◇  K Q J 10 7 4
                    ♣  A K

     ♠  J 4                      N
     ♡  A J 9 7 5 2         W         E
     ◇  A 9                       S
     ♣  7 5 4
```

WEST	NORTH	EAST	SOUTH
–	1◇	Pass	1♠
Pass	3◇	Pass	3NT
End			

You lead ♡7 against South's 3NT and dummy's queen wins the trick. Declarer now plays on diamonds, partner playing high-low, to show two cards, and you win the second round. How will you know what to do next?

B.

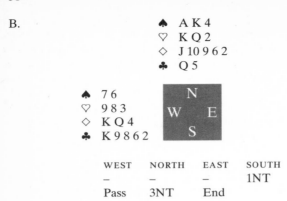

	♠	A K 4
	♡	K Q 2
	◇	J 10 9 6 2
	♣	Q 5

♠	7 6
♡	9 8 3
◇	K Q 4
♣	K 9 8 6 2

WEST	NORTH	EAST	SOUTH
–	–	–	1NT
Pass	3NT	End	

South opens a 12–14 point 1NT and ends in 3NT. You lead ♣6 and dummy's queen wins the trick, the jack falling from South. Declarer runs ◇J to your queen. How will you know what to do next?

C.

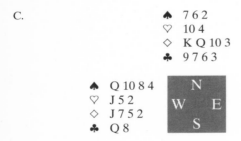

	♠	7 6 2
	♡	10 4
	◇	K Q 10 3
	♣	9 7 6 3

♠	Q 10 8 4
♡	J 5 2
◇	J 7 5 2
♣	Q 8

South opens 2NT and is raised to 3NT. You lead ♠4, drawing the jack from partner and the ace from declarer. Declarer now leads ◇4 from his hand. Which card will you play to this trick? What is the purpose of the card you chose?

ANSWERS

A. The correct defence depends on the count signal your partner gave you in hearts. If he played a low spot-card, there is a fair chance that declarer's king of hearts is now bare and will fall under your ace. You will then be able to run the heart suit. If instead your partner played a high spot-card, showing a doubleton heart, you should switch to a spade. You hope that partner can win with the ace and play a heart through South's king.

B. It seems that declarer started with ♣A J doubleton and a club continuation will now work well. To check on this, look at partner's count signal on the first trick. If he played the 7 (from 10 7 4 3, you hope), go ahead with a second round of clubs. If instead partner played the 3 (from 7 4 3), or the 4 (from 4 3), declarer's jack of clubs must be a false card! Knowing that a second club will run into South's club tenace, you should switch to ♡9. Your aim is to put partner on lead so he can clear the club suit.

C. Declarer is a big favourite to hold the ace of diamonds. If you give a misguided count signal, you will merely assist him to guess the suit correctly when he holds three diamonds to the ace. You should follow with the 2, with the purpose of giving no information away.

5. Tactics at No-trumps

How is your card-play in no-trumps? Are you happy with it? In this chapter we will cover all the basic techniques. By the end, you should know enough to handle at least four no-trump contracts out of five.

Finessing into the safe hand

By way of a refresher, we will start with a fairly easy deal:

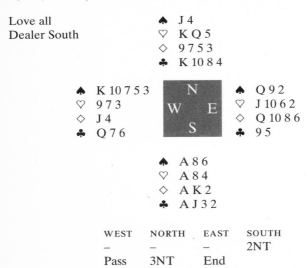

Love all
Dealer South

	♠	J 4
	♡	K Q 5
	◇	9 7 5 3
	♣	K 10 8 4

♠ K 10 7 5 3   ♠ Q 9 2
♡ 9 7 3   ♡ J 10 6 2
◇ J 4   ◇ Q 10 8 6
♣ Q 7 6   ♣ 9 5

	♠	A 8 6
	♡	A 8 4
	◇	A K 2
	♣	A J 3 2

WEST	NORTH	EAST	SOUTH
–	–	–	2NT
Pass	3NT	End	

West leads ♠5. You try your luck with dummy's jack, but East covers with the queen. It is time to employ the most important technique in no-trumps: the hold-up. You allow East's queen to win and play low again when he returns ♠9. What is the purpose of such a hold-up?

You hold up the ace until the third round to exhaust East of his spade holding. It will then be safe to allow him on lead while you establish the nine tricks you need for game. What should you do after winning the third round of spades?

You can count eight top tricks: one spade, three hearts, two diamonds, and two clubs. A ninth trick will have to come from one of the minors. It would be too dangerous to play ace, king and another diamond. Even if the suit broke 3-3 (which is against the odds), West might well win the third round and beat the contract by cashing two spade winners. It is much better to play on clubs, but how should you tackle the suit? If you cross to the king of clubs and finesse the jack, this will be into the dangerous West hand. Instead you should cash the ace of clubs, then finesse dummy's ♣10. No matter if it loses. East will have no spade to return (unless the suit breaks 4-4, when the contract is secure anyway), so you will make the game.

Suppose this was the club holding instead:

```
              ♣  K 10 8 5 4
    ♣  Q 9 7                ♣  6
              ♣  A J 3 2
```

With nine clubs between the hands, you would normally play for the drop. In the context of our present deal, however, you should again finesse into the safe (East) hand. If you played the ace and king of clubs instead, you would go down whenever West held three clubs to the queen.

What if this had been the club position (still with West as the danger hand):

```
              ♣  K 9 6 4
    ♣  Q 8 5                ♣  10 7
              ♣  A J 3 2
```

You should cash the ace of clubs, then lead a low club towards dummy. If West follows with a small card, you cover with dummy's 9. Here the 9 loses to the 10. No problem. East has no spade to play and you will have nine tricks after winning his return.

Playing the ace first will not jeopardise the success of the contract, should East hold the queen:

```
              ♣  K 9 6 4
    ♣  5                    ♣  Q 10 8 7
              ♣  A J 3 2
```

When West shows out on the second round, you rise with dummy's king and lead back towards the jack. You don't mind East (the safe hand) gaining the lead.

We'll change the club suit just one more time:

♣ K 7 6 4

♣ A J 3 2

Again you need to establish a third trick from the clubs without letting West on lead. Any ideas?

It would still be wrong to take a club finesse (which would be into the dangerous hand). You should cash the ace and king, saving the contract when West started with queen doubleton. If both defenders follow but the queen fails to drop, you will play a third round, hoping that East wins the trick. As with the previous combination, you would still score the three tricks you need when East holds four clubs to the queen.

Here is another full deal on this theme:

Love all
Dealer North

		♠	Q 2	
		♡	J 5	
		♢	A K 8 6 4 2	
		♣	K 9 2	

♠ A J 9 6 5	N	♠ 10 8 3
♡ K 7 2	W E	♡ Q 10 6
♢ 9	S	♢ J 7 5 3
♣ J 8 6 5		♣ Q 10 4

	♠	K 7 4
	♡	A 9 8 4 3
	♢	Q 10
	♣	A 7 3

WEST	NORTH	EAST	SOUTH
–	1♢	Pass	1♡
Pass	2♢	Pass	3NT
End			

You arrive in 3NT and West leads ♠6, dummy's queen winning the trick. What would you do at trick 2?

Aiming to keep East (the danger hand) off lead, you should finesse ♢10. As the cards lie, you will score an overtrick. If the diamond finesse had lost, even to a singleton jack, you would still have five diamond tricks, enough for the contract. West, meanwhile, would not be able to play spades effectively from his side of the table. If instead you crossed to the queen of diamonds at trick 2, you would go down. East would gain the lead with his diamond jack and play a spade through your king.

Let's change that diamond suit a bit:

$$\diamond \text{ A K 8 6 4 2}$$
$$\diamond \text{ 10} \qquad \diamond \text{ J 7 5 3}$$
$$\diamond \text{ Q 9}$$

Still needing to keep East off lead, you would lead a low diamond to the 9. The play would fail only when East held J 10 x x (even then, he might be too sleepy to insert a high card!)

Ducking into the safe hand

Sometimes both defenders hold an honour in the suit you are trying to develop. Even when no finessing position is present, you may be able to choose which defender gains the lead.

Let's suppose you cannot afford to let West gain the lead and must develop a third trick from this suit:

$$\diamond \text{ 8 6 5 3}$$
$$\diamond \text{ J 10 4} \qquad \diamond \text{ Q 2}$$
$$\diamond \text{ A K 9 7}$$

It's no good simply cashing the ace and king. West, the danger hand, will win the third round. Instead, you must lead the suit twice from the dummy. If the queen appears from East at any time, you will play low, allowing the safe hand to win the trick. If the queen does not appear from East on either the first or second round, you will score two tricks with the ace and king, then play a third round. All will be well if East has three diamonds, rather than West.

The same play would be successful here:

$$\diamond \text{ 8 6 5}$$
$$\diamond \text{ J 10 4} \qquad \diamond \text{ Q 3 2}$$
$$\diamond \text{ A K 9 7}$$

Again you need to establish an extra diamond trick without allowing West on lead. If you play the ace and king East will have the chance to dispose of the queen, allowing West to win the third round. To prevent this, you must lead the suit twice from dummy. If East plays the queen on either of the first two rounds, you will allow the card to win the trick. If not, the ace and king will win the first two rounds and you will give up a trick to the safe (East) hand on the third round.

Here is a full deal on this theme:

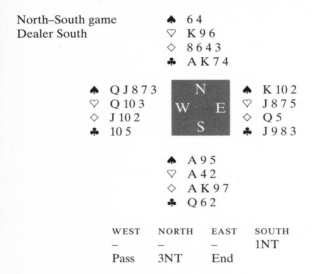

North–South game
Dealer South

		♠	6 4
		♡	K 9 6
		◇	8 6 4 3
		♣	A K 7 4

♠ Q J 8 7 3   ♠ K 10 2
♡ Q 10 3   ♡ J 8 7 5
◇ J 10 2   ◇ Q 5
♣ 10 5   ♣ J 9 8 3

♠ A 9 5
♡ A 4 2
◇ A K 9 7
♣ Q 6 2

WEST	NORTH	EAST	SOUTH
–	–	–	1NT
Pass	3NT	End	

West leads ♠7 against your 3NT contract. East plays the king and you hold up the ace. When East returns ♠10, it seems that the spades are 5-3 (or 6-2). You hold up the ace again and West, on seeing your 9 appear, overtakes and clears the suit. What now?

There is no hurry to try for a 3-3 club break. You will lose nothing by leading twice towards your diamond honours, hoping for the queen to appear from East. Here, the queen will show on the second round. By allowing it to win, you will have your nine tricks. Had the queen not appeared, both defenders following suit, you would test the clubs next. If that suit failed to break 3-3 you would surrender a trick in diamonds, hoping that it was East who held the missing card in that suit. Even if he then had a club to cash, you would make the contract, losing only two spades, one diamond and one club.

The decision to follow such a line of play depended on the assumption that spades were 5-3. Suppose instead that the spades were 4-4, West leading ♠3 to East's king and East returning ♠2. Now you could not afford to test the clubs before clearing the diamond suit. The defenders might then score three spades, one diamond and one club. You would play on diamonds directly, expecting to lose only three spades and one diamond.

Should I hold up from A J x?

Suppose West leads ♡4 and this is the heart position:

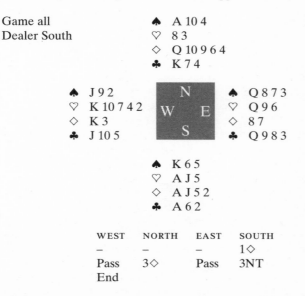

```
                    ♡  8 3
  ♡  K 10 7 4 2              ♡  Q 9 6
                    ♡  A J 5
```

Should you capture East's queen immediately, or hold up? It's a trick question (no pun intended) and you cannot give an answer without looking at the full deal. It depends which defender is likely to gain the lead when you develop the other suits. Suppose this is the lay-out:

Game all
Dealer South

```
                    ♠  A 10 4
                    ♡  8 3
                    ◇  Q 10 9 6 4
                    ♣  K 7 4

  ♠  J 9 2                         ♠  Q 8 7 3
  ♡  K 10 7 4 2     N             ♡  Q 9 6
  ◇  K 3          W     E         ◇  8 7
  ♣  J 10 5         S             ♣  Q 9 8 3

                    ♠  K 6 5
                    ♡  A J 5
                    ◇  A J 5 2
                    ♣  A 6 2
```

WEST	NORTH	EAST	SOUTH
–	–	–	1◇
Pass	3◇	Pass	3NT
End			

West leads ♡4 to East's queen. How will you play 3NT?

You will need to set up the diamond suit. If the diamond finesse loses, it is West who will gain the lead. You should therefore win the first round of hearts with the ace. Even if the diamond finesse fails, you will be safe. With West on lead, your remaining ♡J 5 will guard the suit.

Let's alter the diamond position and see how this affects your play at trick 1:

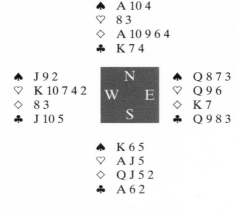

```
            ♠ A 10 4
            ♡ 8 3
            ◇ A 10 9 6 4
            ♣ K 7 4

♠ J 9 2                      ♠ Q 8 7 3
♡ K 10 7 4 2      N          ♡ Q 9 6
◇ 8 3         W       E      ◇ K 7
♣ J 10 5          S          ♣ Q 9 8 3

            ♠ K 6 5
            ♡ A J 5
            ◇ Q J 5 2
            ♣ A 6 2
```

Now the diamond finesse is into the East hand. You would go down if you won the first heart. To make the contract you would have to hold up the ace of hearts for two rounds, exhausting East of the suit. Again the contract will be safe, even if the diamond finesse loses.

The decision – whether or not to hold up – is not so easy on the next deal. Would you have made the contract?

North–South game
Dealer South

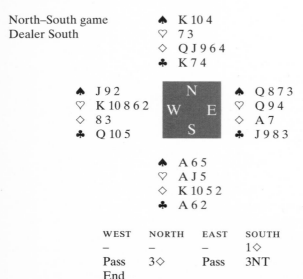

```
            ♠ K 10 4
            ♡ 7 3
            ◇ Q J 9 6 4
            ♣ K 7 4

♠ J 9 2                      ♠ Q 8 7 3
♡ K 10 8 6 2     N           ♡ Q 9 4
◇ 8 3        W       E       ◇ A 7
♣ Q 10 5         S           ♣ J 9 8 3

            ♠ A 6 5
            ♡ A J 5
            ◇ K 10 5 2
            ♣ A 6 2
```

WEST	NORTH	EAST	SOUTH
–	–	–	1◇
Pass	3◇	Pass	3NT
End			

West leads ♡6 against 3NT, East producing the queen. Should you hold up or not? It depends on who holds the ace of diamonds. If West has the ace, you should win the first trick. If East has it, you should hold up for two rounds. There is a small clue to the winning play. Can you spot it?

The contract is in danger only if West holds five or more hearts. If he held the ace of diamonds too, in addition to a possible black-suit card or two, he might have ventured a non-vulnerable overcall of 1♡. Since he did not make a bid, the odds favour East holding the diamond ace. You should therefore hold up in hearts.

Suppose the auction was different and West did venture a 1♡ overcall. The odds would then switch. With West a strong favourite to hold the diamond ace, you would win the first heart – retaining your ♡J 5 as a second stopper.

Hold-up with two stoppers

Suppose West leads a spade against 3NT, the suit lying like this:

```
                ♠ 9 5 3
    ♠ Q 10 8 4 2         ♠ J 6
                ♠ A K 7
```

We'll imagine also that the defenders hold one ace each, both of which will have to be knocked out before you can score nine tricks. If you win the first round of spades and choose to play on the suit where East has the ace, you will go down. He will clear the spades and West will come on lead with the other ace.

To make the contract you must hold up on the first round of spades, even though you have two stoppers in the suit. East will return a spade, but the contract will then be safe. When you knock out East's ace, he will have no spade to return.

Let's see how this works in the context of a full deal.

Love all   ♠ 9 5 3
Dealer South   ♡ Q 9 6
                  ◇ K Q J 3
                  ♣ A Q 4

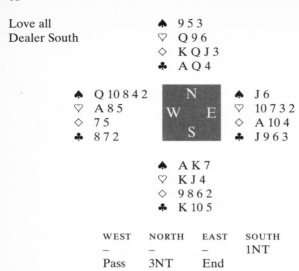

    ♠ Q 10 8 4 2   ♠ J 6
    ♡ A 8 5   ♡ 10 7 3 2
    ◇ 7 5   ◇ A 10 4
    ♣ 8 7 2   ♣ J 9 6 3

                  ♠ A K 7
                  ♡ K J 4
                  ◇ 9 8 6 2
                  ♣ K 10 5

WEST	NORTH	EAST	SOUTH
–	–	–	1NT
Pass	3NT	End	

West leads ♠4, East producing the jack. If you win the trick and choose – unluckily – to play on diamonds, East will pounce with the ace and clear the spade suit. When you seek a ninth trick in hearts, West will take his ace immediately and cash two spade tricks, putting you one down.

See the effect if you hold up at trick one. East returns a spade to your ace but will have no spade to play when he takes the ace of diamonds. You can win his return and knock out the heart ace, still with one stopper to guard the spade suit. Ten tricks.

Suppose this has been the spade lay-out:

              ♠ 9 8 2
   ♠ J 10 6 5 3   ♠ K 4
             ♠ A Q 7

West leads ♠5 and East plays the king. The position is identical, in all respects, to that on the hand we have just seen. Nevertheless, it's surprising how many players have a blind-spot with this combination, failing to hold up when they should have done.

Which side suit should I play first?

We will now look at some hands where you need to play on two suits to bring your total to nine tricks. Some thought may be required before deciding which side suit to attack first.

You will often encounter deals of this type:

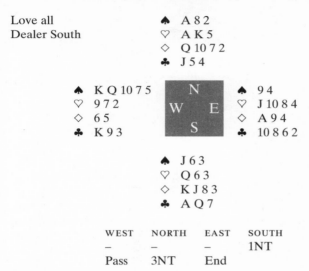

Love all   ♠ A 8 2
Dealer South   ♡ A K 5
                ◇ Q 10 7 2
                ♣ J 5 4

♠ K Q 10 7 5   ♠ 9 4
♡ 9 7 2   ♡ J 10 8 4
◇ 6 5   ◇ A 9 4
♣ K 9 3   ♣ 10 8 6 2

                ♠ J 6 3
                ♡ Q 6 3
                ◇ K J 8 3
                ♣ A Q 7

WEST	NORTH	EAST	SOUTH
–	–	–	1NT
Pass	3NT	End	

West leads the king of spades. How would you plan to make nine tricks?

The first move is to allow West's king to win. He cannot then continue the suit without giving you two spade tricks. Let's say he switches to a heart. What now?

Suppose you win and play on diamonds next. East will rise with the ace and clear the spade suit. When you subsequently seek a ninth trick by taking a club finesse, West will win and cash two spades to put the game one down. (At double-dummy, you could make the contract by winning the second spade and eventually end-playing West, but this would require some good guesswork.)

A much better idea is to play on clubs before diamonds. Do you see why? Because if a club to the queen loses, West will be on lead; he will still not be able to clear the spade suit. With a second club trick established, you will win West's return and knock out the ace of diamonds. Nine tricks made.

On the next deal you have finesses to take in hearts and diamonds. You must decide which finesse to take first.

Love all   ♠ A 8 7
Dealer South   ♡ A Q 9 3
                      ◇ J 10 4 3
                      ♣ A 4

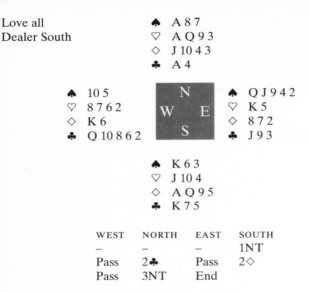

♠ 10 5	♠ Q J 9 4 2
♡ 8 7 6 2	♡ K 5
◇ K 6	◇ 8 7 2
♣ Q 10 8 6 2	♣ J 9 3

                      ♠ K 6 3
                      ♡ J 10 4
                      ◇ A Q 9 5
                      ♣ K 7 5

WEST	NORTH	EAST	SOUTH
–	–	–	1NT
Pass	2♣	Pass	2◇
Pass	3NT	End	

West leads ♣6 against your 3NT. What is the safe route to nine tricks? If either red-suit king is onside, you will make four tricks from that suit – enough for the contract. You should therefore plan the play on the assumption that both kings are offside. Which finesse do you think you should take first in this case?

The rule on these hands is to attack first the entry to the hand with the long suit (here clubs). When you subsequently play on the suit where the other defender may hold a stopper, he will have no clubs left.

Here you must take the diamond finesse first. You win the club lead with dummy's ace and run the jack of diamonds. It loses to the king and West returns a club. You hold up the king, aiming to leave East with no clubs, and win the third round of the suit. It is now safe to take the heart finesse. If it loses, East will have no club to return (or clubs will break 4-4, when you will lose only two clubs and the two red-suit kings).

Perhaps you wondered why it was right to win the first round of clubs on that deal, rather than hold up. The reason is that a hold-up on the first round would give the defenders a chance to switch to spades. You would then be at risk of losing tricks in spades, as well as the two red-suit kings and one trick already conceded in clubs. By winning the first round of clubs, you keep the defenders' spades out of the picture.

Let's change the deal a little, moving the ace of clubs to the South hand:

```
              ♠ A 8 7
              ♡ A Q 9 3
              ◇ J 10 4 3
              ♣ 7 4

  ♠ 10 5           N          ♠ Q J 9 4 2
  ♡ 8 7 6 2                   ♡ K 5
  ◇ K 6      W         E      ◇ 8 7 2
  ♣ Q 10 8 6 2    S          ♣ J 9 3

              ♠ K 6 3
              ♡ J 10 4
              ◇ A Q 9 5
              ♣ A K 5
```

West leads ♣6 against your 3NT. You win East's jack with the ace and, as before, want to play on diamonds before hearts. How can you reach dummy, though, to take the diamond finesse? If you cross to ♠A, West can clear the spade suit when he wins with the diamond king. Do you see what you should do?

Since you can afford the diamond finesse to lose, there is no reason not to lead diamonds from the South hand! You play the ace of diamonds, followed by the queen. West wins and plays another club. You hold up the king and win the third round of clubs. East has no clubs left now, so it will be safe to take a heart finesse into his hand. Ten tricks will result.

Avoidance play

We'll end the chapter with something a bit more exotic. Suppose you need an extra trick from each of two suits and have only one stopper left in the defenders' suit. This is one of the suits from which you need an extra trick:

```
              ◇ Q 6 3
  ◇ 10 8 5              ◇ A J 9 4
              ◇ K 7 2
```

If you play a low diamond to the queen, East will win and clear the defenders' long suit. It will then be too late to set up the extra trick you need from your other side suit. Suppose, instead, that you lead a low diamond from dummy – through East's high card. If he rises with the ace, you will score two diamond tricks – enough for the contract. If instead East ducks, you will score a trick with the diamond king and still have time to play on the second suit.

It's a slightly complicated idea and it will help us to look at a full deal:

Love all
Dealer East

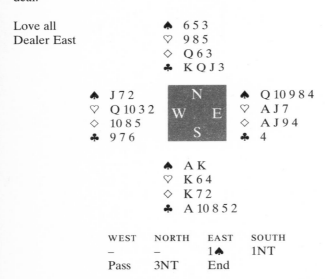

	♠ 6 5 3	
	♡ 9 8 5	
	◇ Q 6 3	
	♣ K Q J 3	
♠ J 7 2		♠ Q 10 9 8 4
♡ Q 10 3 2		♡ A J 7
◇ 10 8 5		◇ A J 9 4
♣ 9 7 6		♣ 4
	♠ A K	
	♡ K 6 4	
	◇ K 7 2	
	♣ A 10 8 5 2	

WEST	NORTH	EAST	SOUTH
–	–	1♠	1NT
Pass	3NT	End	

West leads ♠2 against 3NT. How can you score nine tricks before East scores five?

There are seven top tricks available in the black suits, so you need to build two more tricks in the red suits. If you play a diamond to the queen, East will win and clear the spade suit. The defenders will score five tricks before you can make a trick with the heart king. The same fate awaits if you cross to a club and lead a heart. East will rise with the ace and clear the spade suit, holding you to eight tricks.

Instead, you should cross to dummy with a club and lead a diamond towards your hand. If East rises with the ace now, you will have two diamond tricks – for a total of nine. If East chooses to play low on the first round of diamonds, you will pocket your trick in that suit, return to dummy with a club, and lead a heart towards the king. Nine tricks are assured.

See if you can spot a similar play on this deal:

North–South game
Dealer East

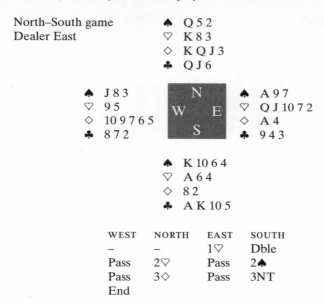

♠ Q 5 2
♡ K 8 3
♢ K Q J 3
♣ Q J 6

♠ J 8 3
♡ 9 5
♢ 10 9 7 6 5
♣ 8 7 2

♠ A 9 7
♡ Q J 10 7 2
♢ A 4
♣ 9 4 3

♠ K 10 6 4
♡ A 6 4
♢ 8 2
♣ A K 10 5

WEST	NORTH	EAST	SOUTH
–	–	1♡	Dble
Pass	2♡	Pass	2♠
Pass	3♢	Pass	3NT
End			

You reach 3NT after East has opened the bidding in hearts. West leads ♡9. How can you make nine tricks?

Suppose you win the heart lead and play on diamonds. East will win with the ace and clear the heart suit. When you seek a ninth trick in spades East will take three heart tricks, putting the game one down.

To have any chance of making nine tricks you must play on spades first. You win the heart lead with dummy's king. (There is no point in a hold-up, because you know from the bidding that East will hold the two missing aces.) You then lead a small spade from dummy, through East's ace. If East plays his ace on dummy's 2, he will pay heavily for the privilege. He will give you three spade tricks – enough for the contract! If instead he plays low, you will win the trick with the king. Now you can turn to the diamond suit, bumping your total to nine tricks.

The last two hands have been examples of what is known as 'avoidance play'. By leading a low card through a defender's stopper, you make him pay a high price for taking a trick with it.

POINTS TO REMEMBER

1. When one of the defenders (known as the 'danger hand') has winners to cash, you must aim to keep him off lead while you establish the tricks you need.

2. You should usually take finesses into the 'safe hand', even on combinations where you would normally play for the drop or finesse the other way.

3. When you have two stoppers to knock out, you should usually attack first the stopper that lies with the enemy long suit. Your hope is that the other defender will have no cards left in that suit by the time you knock out his stopper.

4. It may pay you to hold up in the enemy suit even when you have two stoppers there. This is likely to be the case when the defenders have two high cards that you must knock out.

5. By leading a low card through an enemy top card, you can sometimes give the defender no winning option. If he rises, he will give you an extra trick. If he ducks, you will win the trick and switch to a different suit.

TEST YOURSELF

A.

```
              ♠  6 3
              ♡  K Q 8 4
              ◇  K 6 2
              ♣  A J 9 3

                    N
    ♠7 led    W           E
                    S

              ♠  K Q 8
              ♡  A 7 2
              ◇  A 9 7 3
              ♣  Q 10 2
```

WEST	NORTH	EAST	SOUTH
–	–	–	1◇
1♠	Dble	Pass	1NT
Pass	3NT	End	

Your partner makes a negative (take-out) double on the first round and you end in 3NT. West leads ♠7 and East plays the 10. Plan the play.

B.

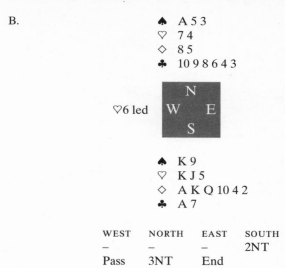

♠ A 5 3
♡ 7 4
◇ 8 5
♣ 10 9 8 6 4 3

♡6 led

♠ K 9
♡ K J 5
◇ A K Q 10 4 2
♣ A 7

WEST	NORTH	EAST	SOUTH
–	–	–	2NT
Pass	3NT	End	

West leads ♡6 against your 3NT contract, East producing the queen. How will you play the hand?

C.

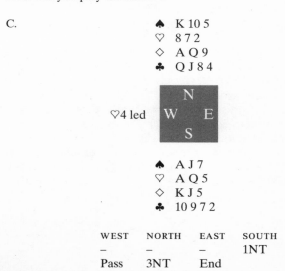

♠ K 10 5
♡ 8 7 2
◇ A Q 9
♣ Q J 8 4

♡4 led

♠ A J 7
♡ A Q 5
◇ K J 5
♣ 10 9 7 2

WEST	NORTH	EAST	SOUTH
–	–	–	1NT
Pass	3NT	End	

West leads ♡4 against your 3NT contract, East producing the king. How will you play the hand?

D.

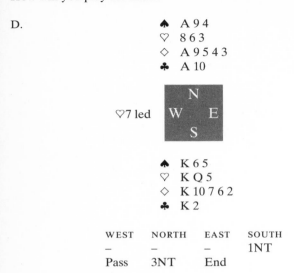

♠ A 9 4
♡ 8 6 3
◇ A 9 5 4 3
♣ A 10

♡7 led

♠ K 6 5
♡ K Q 5
◇ K 10 7 6 2
♣ K 2

WEST	NORTH	EAST	SOUTH
–	–	–	1NT
Pass	3NT	End	

West leads ♡7 against 3NT, East playing the 10. Against which lie of the diamond suit will it be right to win the first heart trick? How would the diamonds need to lie for a hold-up in hearts to be beneficial? Which of these two diamond positions is more likely? And how will you therefore play the contract?

ANSWERS

A. The key finesse, in clubs, is into the East hand. You must therefore aim to exhaust East of spades before you take the finesse. Duck the first round of spades. If spades are 6-2, the link will be broken between the two defenders, whether or not West takes his ace on the second round of spades. If spades are 5-3, and the club finesse is wrong, you cannot make the contract anyway. West will retain communications by holding up the spade ace until the third round.

B. You should win the first round of hearts with the king. Suppose you now cash two top diamonds and find that East started with four to the jack. Unless the hearts are 4-4, which is unlikely, you will be one down. When you concede a diamond trick to East, he will play a heart through the jack. Instead you should cash one top diamond, then cross to dummy's ♠A to finesse ◇10 into the safe (West) hand. You will make the contract whether the finesse succeeds or not.

C. You need to establish two club tricks. Suppose you win the first heart and play on clubs. East may win the first round of clubs and clear the heart suit. If West then wins the next round of clubs, you may lose three hearts and two clubs. To prevent this, you should duck the first round of hearts. If East continues hearts, and the suit breaks 5-2, he will have no heart to play when he gains the lead in clubs. If hearts are 4-3 the contract will succeed anyway.

D. If you win the first heart, East becomes the danger hand. You will go down when East has ◇Q J x and can play a second heart through. If you duck the first heart, the defenders will clear the heart suit and West will become the danger hand. You will then go down when West holds ◇Q J x. Since West holds five hearts to East's two, in the dangerous case, it is more likely that East has ◇Q J x than West. You should therefore hold up at trick 1.

6. Directing the Opening Lead

The opponents reach a game or slam and partner is on lead. You have something good in diamonds and are praying that a diamond will appear on the table. No, partner leads a club and declarer soon makes the contract. We have all suffered a similar fate, many times over. Sometimes, though, the auction offers a chance to tell partner which suit you would like him to lead. In this chapter we will see the various ways it can be done.

Directing the lead with an overcall

One of the main reasons for making an overcall is to suggest a good opening lead to partner. It is sometimes worth putting your head on the block to pass this message.

West	North	East	South	WEST
–	1◇	Pass	1♡	♠ 6 3
?				♡ J 9 6 3
				◇ A 5
				♣ K Q J 8 4

Suppose you pass and the bidding continues with 1NT by North and 3NT by South. Partner will lead a spade, won't he? What's more he will look accusingly at you when you can only produce the 6! You can avoid such a fate by overcalling 2♣ on hands like this. Many tournament players would risk the bid, even when vulnerable against not. Dangerous, yes, but the benefits of an eventual club lead are worth paying for.

What bid would you choose on the West cards here:

West	North	East	South	WEST
–	1♣	Pass	1◇	♠ A K Q 7 3
?				♡ J 8 6 5 4
				◇ 9
				♣ 10 5

Since you hold both the unbid suits, you might consider a take-out double. It is much better to overcall 1♠. If the opponents win the auction and your partner is on lead, he will then lead a spade rather than a heart. If instead the opponents' bidding stops low (if North's rebid of 2♣ or 2♢ is followed by two passes, for example), you can contest further with 2♡.

Switch the major suits round, giving you ♡AKQ73 and five moderate spades, you would then overcall in hearts, the suit you want to be led. If North's rebid of 2♣ or 2♢ ran round to you, you could compete further with a take-out double – showing that you had length in spades too.

Opening in the third seat to direct a lead

It is a popular tactic to open light in the third position, to disrupt the opponents' bidding. When you are considering a borderline third-seat opening on some 10 points or so, look at the quality of the suit you will be bidding. If you will be happy to see partner lead this suit, should the opponents win the auction, go ahead with your opening bid.

Suppose, after two passes and with the score at Love all, you hold one of the following hands. Would you open the bidding?

	(1)		(2)		(3)
♠	J 8 7 6 2	♠	K Q J 7 3	♠	A 4
♡	K Q 5	♡	7 2	♡	8 2
♢	J 4	♢	A 10 4	♢	K Q J 10 7 3
♣	A 7 2	♣	9 8 2	♣	J 6 4

With such a poor suit, there's little to be gained by opening 1♠ on (1). If your partner ends up on lead and strikes out with the spade ace or king, you will regret opening your mouth. Hand (2) is different. The spades demand to be mentioned and you should open 1♠ or a weak 2♠. With (3) the best opening in third seat is 3♢. You want a diamond lead, yes, but you also want to make it difficult for the opponents to enter in the majors.

Directing the lead by doubling a conventional bid

When the opponents have made an artificial bid, you may be able to double to suggest an opening lead. How do you and your partner treat a double of a Stayman bid in this sequence:

WEST	NORTH	EAST	SOUTH
1NT	Pass	2♣	Dble

There are two possible meanings of the double: clubs, or general strength. Against a weak 1NT (12–14 points), most tournament players use a double to indicate strength. They would double with upwards of 15 points, showing a hand strong enough for a penalty double of 1NT. This is the only effective counter against opponents who bid Stayman on very weak hands.

When 1NT is strong, however, or when South is a passed hand, a double should show a strong holding in clubs. You are not so much suggesting that partner should contest in clubs, if he has a fit there, more that he should lead a club against the eventual contract by the opponents.

The same is true when the opponents use a transfer response:

WEST	NORTH	EAST	SOUTH
1NT	Pass	2◇ (1)	Dble

(1) Transfer bid, showing hearts

Again the double should merely show a strong hand when 1NT is weak. If 1NT is strong, or South has already passed, the double should direct partner to a diamond lead.

When the opponents have opened with some strong bid at the two level, all doubles of artificial bids will be lead-directional:

WEST	NORTH	EAST	SOUTH
2♣	Dble		

The double shows strong clubs. You would double on ♣K Q J 9 4, for example. With six or seven good clubs, you would be more inclined to actually bid the suit, to deny the opponents bidding space.

The situation is similar after an artificial negative response:

WEST	NORTH	EAST	SOUTH
2♣	Pass	2◇	Dble

South's double shows good diamonds.

You can make the same type of double when an opponent has opened 2NT:

WEST	NORTH	EAST	SOUTH
2NT	Pass	3♣	Dble

South doubles the Stayman call to show something good in clubs. Had he doubled a transfer response of 3◇ or 3♡, he would again show values in the suit artificially bid.

Another important opportunity arises when the opponents use the 'fourth suit forcing' method.

West	North	East	South	WEST
–	1♠	Pass	2♣	♠ 6
Pass	2♡	Pass	3◇	♡ J 9 6 3
?				◇ K Q 10 8 5
				♣ J 8 4

Sitting West, you should double the fourth-suit bid of 3◇. Partner would tend to lead the unbid diamond suit anyway, it's true, but he might be nervous to lead from such as ◇J x or ◇J x x. There's no harm in making sure.

When you have already bid a suit, and an opponent subsequently makes a strength-showing cue-bid there, you have the opportunity to confirm that you would like your suit led.

West	North	East	South	WEST
1♠	2♣	Pass	2♠	♠ K Q J 9 4
?				♡ A J 7
				◇ K 10 5 3
				♣ 4

Here you double, telling partner that you would like a spade lead. With such as ♠A 10 8 6 5 you would pass, letting partner know that your spades were not particularly strong and it might be better to lead a different suit.

When the opponents are heading for a slam, there will be frequent opportunities for a lead-directing double. You can double a Blackwood response or a control-showing cue-bid.

West	North	East	South	WEST
–	–	–	1NT	♠ 6 2
Pass	3♠	Pass	4♣	♡ Q 5 4
?				◇ J 5
				♣ Q 10 9 8 6 2

South's 4♣ agrees spades as trumps and shows a control (ace or king) in clubs. A double by you would suggest a club opening lead. Should you double? Not on this hand, since you have no particular reason to think that a club lead is best. If partner's normal lead would be in one of the red suits, that might work equally well. If you held only small cards in the red suits, you would be more inclined to double for a club lead.

Inferences may sometimes be drawn when partner does *not* make a lead-directing double. Take the West cards below and decide what you would lead against South's 6♠.

West	North	East	South	WEST	
–	2♣	Pass	2♠	♠	6
Pass	3♠	Pass	4NT	♡	10 8 6 3
Pass	5♢	Pass	6♠	♢	9 7 4 2
End				♣	J 8 6 3

It's unattractive to lead either of the black suits. Which red suit should you choose? If partner held something good in diamonds, such as ♢K Q 8 3, he might have doubled the 5♢ Blackwood response. It is therefore more likely that a heart lead will be productive.

Doubling 3NT for a lead

Suppose you have bid a suit and the opponents subsequently reach 3NT. If you double this contract, the message will be: Lead my suit and the contract will go down! This might be the situation:

West	North	East	South	EAST	
–	–	1♢	1NT	♠	6
Pass	3NT	?		♡	A 3 2
				♢	K Q J 10 4
				♣	K J 7 4

If you pass now, expecting partner to lead the suit you have bid, you may be disappointed. If partner holds a singleton diamond, he may look favourably on his ♠Q 10 8 5 3 and place ♠5 on the table. After winning the spade lead and dislodging your ♡A, declarer might well have nine tricks at his disposal. To force partner to lead a diamond, you should double.

Sometimes you hold a good suit but the opponents shoot into 3NT before you have a chance to bid. There is little hope that partner, unprompted, will choose to lead your suit. You can alert him to the situation by doubling 3NT. Such a double is conventional and means 'I have an excellent suit. Please try to find it.' Normally, partner will then lead his weakest suit.

West	North	East	South	EAST
–	–	–	1NT	♠ A Q J 10 7
Pass	3NT	?		♡ 5 2
				◇ A 4
				♣ 10 9 4 3

East doubles, hoping that his partner will now find a spade lead. Such a double asks for a major-suit lead more often than not. That's because the responder (North, here) would usually have bid Stayman if he held a major suit himself.

Such doubles carry an element of risk, because a 1NT–3NT auction is limited only by responder's failure to investigate a slam. Once in a while, the responder will have points to spare for his raise and will punish you with a redouble. It's a price worth paying. Most bridge actions carry an element of risk.

When dummy has bid a suit, but neither defender has bid, a double of 3NT suggests the lead of dummy's suit:

West	North	East	South	EAST
–	1♡	Pass	1NT	♠ 6 2
Pass	2NT	Pass	3NT	♡ A J 10 9 4
Pass	Pass	?		◇ A Q 2
				♣ 8 5 3

East should double, to suggest a heart lead. The contract is clearly more likely to fail after a heart lead than any other. Here the opponents' auction is limited, so there is not much risk attached to the double.

Lightner doubles

Easily the most famous lead-directing bid is the Lightner Slam Double. When the opponents have reached a freely bid slam, it is scarcely worth using a double for penalties – seeking to convert +50 into +100, or +100 into +200. Realising this, Theodore Lightner suggested that such a double should suggest an unusual opening lead. The gain is spectacular when the mechanism succeeds and a horrendous −980 or −1430 is transformed into a plus score.

What does 'unusual lead' mean, in this context? Often the doubler will be void in a suit. The player on lead must guess which suit this is, from the bidding and from his own length in the various suits. What would you lead here?

West	North	East	South		WEST
–	–	Pass	1♠	♠	6
Pass	3♡	Pass	3♠	♡	J 9 7 5 3
Pass	4♠	Pass	4NT	◇	J 10 4
Pass	5◇	Pass	6♠	♣	Q 10 7 4
Pass	Pass	Dble	End		

Without partner's double, you would surely have led one of the minors. You would perhaps have preferred a club because partner spurned the chance to make a lead-directing double of the 5◇ Blackwood response. Everything changes when partner makes a Lightner double. There would be nothing 'unexpected' about a club or diamond lead. Partner is probably void in hearts and that is the suit you should lead.

Many partnerships have the understanding that a Lightner double will never request the lead of a suit that has been bid by the defenders. Suppose, for example, that your partner has opened 3♠ and will be on lead against the opponent's small slam in diamonds. If you were void in spades, you would not make a Lightner Double. Partner will usually have a respectable spade suit for his opening bid and it would not be 'unexpected' for him to lead a spade.

Lead-directing bids in competitive auctions

When the auction is competitive, and you have already found a trump fit, you can sometimes make a lead-directing bid in a new suit rather than bidding the agreed trump suit again. See what you make of the following deal:

Dealer East
Love all

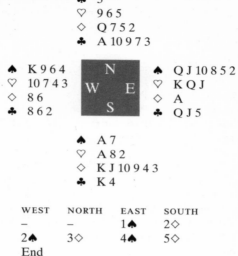

```
                      ♠ 3
                      ♡ 9 6 5
                      ◇ Q 7 5 2
                      ♣ A 10 9 7 3

   ♠ K 9 6 4          N          ♠ Q J 10 8 5 2
   ♡ 10 7 4 3      W     E       ♡ K Q J
   ◇ 8 6              S          ◇ A
   ♣ 8 6 2                       ♣ Q J 5

                      ♠ A 7
                      ♡ A 8 2
                      ◇ K J 10 9 4 3
                      ♣ K 4
```

WEST	NORTH	EAST	SOUTH
–	–	1♠	2◇
2♠	3◇	4♠	5◇
End			

West led ♠4 and declarer won the trick with the ace. He knocked out the ace of trumps, won the heart return, and drew trumps. It was then a simple matter to set up the club suit, return to dummy with a spade ruff, and discard his two heart losers on the good clubs.

'Should we have been in the slam?' asked North.

'I go down in Five Diamonds on a heart lead,' his partner replied.

Do you see how East could have suggested a heart lead? Instead of rebidding 4♠, he should have said 4♡. This could scarcely be a slam try, after his partner's single raise. West should read such a bid as lead-directional.

POINTS TO REMEMBER

1. Look out for opportunities to suggest a good opening lead to your partner. You can do this by overcalling, also by doubling artificial bids by the opponents.

2. Lead-directing doubles can be made over various bids by the opponents: Stayman, transfer bids, fourth-suit forcing bids, strength-showing cue-bids, Blackwood responses, and control-showing cue-bids.

3. The Lightner double of a slam asks partner to find an unusual lead. The required lead will often be the first suit bid by the dummy, never a suit that has been bid by the defenders.

TEST YOURSELF

A.

West	North	East	South	WEST	
–	–	1♠	Dble	♠	4
Pass	2♠	Dble	3♣	♡	K 5
Pass	3♡	Pass	3NT	◇	Q J 9 8 6 5
End				♣	9 8 6 3

What do you understand by your partner's double of North's strength-showing 2♠ cue-bid? What will you lead against South's 3NT?

B.

West	North	East	South	WEST	
–	–	–	1♠	♠	6 4
Pass	3♣	Pass	4♣	♡	K 8 7
Pass	4NT	Pass	5◇	◇	J 10 7 5 3 2
?				♣	J 6

The opponents are heading for a club slam and South has just made a one-ace response to partner's Blackwood. Will you double 5◇ or not?

C.

West	North	East	South	WEST	
–	1♡	Pass	1♠	♠	6 4
Pass	3♠	Pass	4♣	♡	10 8 7 3
Pass	4NT	Pass	5◇	◇	K Q 10 8 5
?				♣	J 6

South has made a control-showing cue-bid in clubs, then shown one ace in response to North's Blackwood call. Should you double this response or not? (Remember what the purpose of such a double is.)

D.	West	North	East	South		WEST
	–	–	–	1♠	♠	A 4
	Pass	3♣	Pass	4♣	♡	J 10 6
	Pass	4♠	Pass	4NT	♢	10 9 7 3
	Pass	5♢	Pass	6♠	♣	10 8 3 2
	End					

What would you lead against South's small slam in spades? Are there any clues hidden in the auction?

ANSWERS

A. Partner's double of the artificial cue-bid shows a strong suit that he would like you to lead. Without the double, you might well have tried your luck with a diamond lead. After partner's double, you should lead your singleton spade.

B. You should not double. Although your diamonds are long, they are headed only by the J 10 and you have no reason at all to favour a diamond lead. In fact, it is more likely that a heart will work better. Even if the diamonds were as strong as Q J 9 x x x, it would be better to pass, leaving partner a free choice between the red suits.

C. The purpose of such a double is to ask partner to lead a diamond. Since you will on lead yourself, against a spade contract, there is little to be gained by doubling 5♢. Indeed, by doing so you might assist declarer in his eventual play of the contract.

D. If you were going to lead a red suit, you would choose a heart. That's because partner might have doubled 5♢ with something good in that suit. Here, however, the opponents have bid and supported clubs and the chances are excellent that they hold at least eight clubs between them. Lead a club, hoping to give partner a club ruff when you win with the trump ace. (You didn't like the trick question? Sorry about that!)

7. Playing the Right Card from Equals

When you hold two or more touching honours, such as the king and queen, you may think that it scarcely matters which one you play. Not so, the contract may depend on your choice! By playing the 'wrong' card, you can give vital information away.

Look at this common situation:

$$\diamond \ 9 \ 7 \ 4$$
$$\diamond \ 8 \ 3 \qquad\qquad \diamond \ K \ 10 \ 6 \ 5 \ 2$$
$$\diamond \ A \ Q \ J$$

East gains the lead and switches to ◇5. Time and again you will see declarers playing the jack, as if it were the normal play. But when the jacks wins, of course, East knows that declarer started with A Q J. If declarer had won with a more sensible queen, East would not know where the jack was. He might persist with the suit later, when a switch elsewhere would have been productive.

This position is similar:

$$\diamond \ 7 \ 5 \ 4$$
$$\diamond \ K \ 9 \ 8 \ 6 \ 3 \qquad\qquad \diamond \ 10 \ 2$$
$$\diamond \ A \ Q \ J$$

West leads ◇6 against a no-trump contract and East plays the 10. If declarer thoughtlessly wins with the jack, West will know that he cannot safely continue the suit when he gains the lead. Declarer should win with the queen, leaving open the possibility (in West's eyes) that East has played the 10 from J 10 or J 10 2.

Touching honours – defending in third seat

The general rule, when defending in the third seat, is to play the lower or lowest of equal cards. The purpose is to inform partner how the suit lies. Suppose that partner leads ♡2 against a suit contract:

$\heartsuit$ 8 6 3

$\heartsuit$ K 10 7 2 $\heartsuit$ Q J 5

$\heartsuit$ A 9 4

When you play the jack and this forces the ace, partner can tell that you hold the queen (otherwise declarer would have won with the queen). He will know that he can safely continue the suit later. Suppose instead that it was your custom to play the top card – here, the queen. When the queen forced the ace, your partner would have no idea where the jack was.

Knowing that partner would play the recommended 'low from equals' can help you to read the cards when he does not hold touching honours. Suppose you are West here:

$\heartsuit$ 8 7

$\heartsuit$ K 10 6 2 $\heartsuit$ Q 9 4 3

$\heartsuit$ A J 5

You lead $\heartsuit$2 and partner's queen forces the ace. Since East would have played the jack from queen-jack, you can place this card with declarer. Unless there is some reason to read South for A J doubleton, a continuation of the suit will not be safe.

It is the same when you hold an interior sequence in third seat:

$\spadesuit$ Q 8 6

$\spadesuit$ J 7 4 3 $\spadesuit$ K 10 9

$\spadesuit$ A 5 2

Partner leads $\spadesuit$3 and declarer plays low from dummy. You should play the 9 rather than the 10. When the 9 forces the ace partner will know that you hold the 10 and that he can safely continue the suit later.

This is the matching situation:

$\spadesuit$ Q 8 6

$\spadesuit$ J 7 4 3 $\spadesuit$ K 10 5

$\spadesuit$ A 9 2

Your $\spadesuit$3 draws the 6, 10 and ace. Partner has denied the 9. It will not be safe for you to continue the suit when you regain the lead.

Look back at the last four positions. When East played 'low from equals', West was able to read all four of them correctly. Playing 'high from equals' would always have left West in doubt. Case proved!

When you are third to play and sitting under the dummy, you will generally win the trick as cheaply as possible.

$$\diamond \quad 7\,6\,4$$
$$\diamond \quad K\,Q\,3 \qquad\qquad \diamond \quad 9\,8\,2$$
$$\diamond \quad A\,J\,10\,5$$

Partner switches to ♢8 (a high spot-card to deny an honour). When the jack is played you should win with the queen. Winning with the king would deny possession of the queen.

Touching honours – defending in second seat

Suppose you are East here:

$$\spadesuit \quad 7\,6$$
$$\spadesuit \quad 9\,8\,5\,3 \qquad\qquad \spadesuit \quad K\,Q\,10\,4$$
$$\spadesuit \quad A\,J\,2$$

Declarer leads a spade from dummy and you decide to rise with an honour. Which card should you play, the higher or the lower of the touching cards?

In the previous section we saw that there was a clear technical advantage in playing the lower of touching honours in third seat. That's why all players use this method. When you rise with an honour in second seat, there is no definite advantage in playing either the higher or the lower honour. Suppose you have agreed to play high; when partner sees the king, he will expect you to have the queen. Suppose instead that you have agreed to play low. When partner sees the queen he will expect you to hold the king. That's because you would normally play 'second hand low' if you held only one honour.

Most players prefer to play the top card from touching honours. The advantage comes when you hold three touching honours. Suppose you hold K Q J 5 in the second seat. If you have agreed to play high and put in the king, partner will know that you have the queen but will be unaware of the jack's position. If you have agreed to play low and put in the jack, partner will know that you have the queen but won't know about the king. The king is a more important card to know about than a jack, which gives a slight edge to playing the top honour in second seat. It is something you should discuss with your partner. ·

Touching honours – defending in fourth seat

The general rule, when defending in fourth seat, is to win the trick as cheaply as possible. We looked at this diamond position a moment or two ago. Suppose now that it is declarer who leads the suit, playing the 4 from dummy.

$$\diamond \ 7\,6\,4$$
$$\diamond \ K\,Q\,3 \qquad \diamond \ 9\,8\,2$$
$$\diamond \ A\,J\,10\,5$$

When declarer plays the jack, you would normally win with the queen, letting partner know that you might hold the king too. If your intention was to mislead the declarer, however, you might choose to win with the king instead.

Touching honours – when playing the contract

As declarer, your sole intention when playing from equals will be to mislead the defenders, or at any rate to give them a guess.

This is a typical position:

$$\clubsuit \ 9\,7$$
$$\clubsuit \ A\,10\,8\,5\,2 \qquad \clubsuit \ J\,6\,4$$
$$\clubsuit \ K\,Q\,3$$

You are playing in a no-trump contract and West leads ♣5, East rising with the jack. If you win with the queen, this is as good as telling West that you also hold the king (since East would have played the king if he held it). When West subsequently gains the lead he may seek an entry to his partner's hand, so a club can be played through your king.

Suppose instead that you win the first trick with the king. Now it will be more difficult for West. He may be tempted to continue clubs, hoping that his partner holds the queen.

We saw in the introduction to this chapter that you would make a similar play from A Q J. You would win the 10 with the queen, keeping the opening leader in the dark as to the position of the jack. The general rule, then, is to play high from equals as declarer. One exception to the rule is worth noting:

◇ 8 3

◇ J 10 7 6 2   ◇ Q 9 5

◇ A K 4

West leads ◇6 against a no-trump contract, East playing the queen. If you win with the ace, the defenders will ask themselves: 'Why on earth didn't he hold up?' They will deduce, rightly, that you must hold the king too. Win instead with the king and you will at least prevent East from knowing the situation. If he gains the lead before his partner, he may persevere with diamonds when you were unprotected in some other suit.

Even when you are not expecting to win the trick, it can be beneficial to play the higher card from touching honours. Look at this deal:

Game all
Dealer South

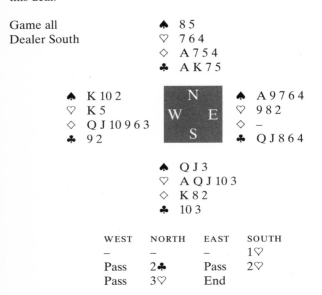

```
                        ♠  8 5
                        ♡  7 6 4
                        ◇  A 7 5 4
                        ♣  A K 7 5

        ♠  K 10 2              N        ♠  A 9 7 6 4
        ♡  K 5             W       E    ♡  9 8 2
        ◇  Q J 10 9 6 3        S        ◇  —
        ♣  9 2                          ♣  Q J 8 6 4

                        ♠  Q J 3
                        ♡  A Q J 10 3
                        ◇  K 8 2
                        ♣  10 3
```

WEST	NORTH	EAST	SOUTH
–	–	–	1♡
Pass	2♣	Pass	2♡
Pass	3♡	End	

West leads ◇Q and is gratified to see his partner ruff. Seeking a second ruff, East returns ♠6. Suppose declarer plays an ingenuous jack on this trick. When West wins with the king, East will know that declarer holds the spade queen. After the second diamond ruff, there will be no temptation to seek a third ruff by underleading the ace of spades again. East will cash the spade ace and West's king of trumps will eventually score the setting trick.

Suppose instead that declarer rises with the queen of spades at trick 2. Now East will have a guess to make after taking his second diamond ruff. If West holds the jack of spades (and no trump trick, holding the queen instead of the king), the only way to beat the contract will be for East to cross once again in spades for a third ruff. Who can blame East if he gets it wrong?

The purpose of 'high from equals, as declarer' is to disguise your strength in the suit led. When you are weak, you may wish to give the opposite impression – feigning strength.

```
Love all                  ♠  J 7 2
Dealer South              ♡  A Q 4 2
                          ◇  9 3
                          ♣  J 9 8 3

        ♠ 10 9 5 4           N           ♠  K Q 8
        ♡ 9 5          W           E     ♡  J 10 8 7
        ◇ A 10 8 6 2                      ◇  J 7 5 4
        ♣ K 7                S           ♣  6 4

                          ♠  A 6 3
                          ♡  K 6 3
                          ◇  K Q
                          ♣  A Q 10 5 2
```

WEST	NORTH	EAST	SOUTH
–	–	–	1♣
Pass	1♡	Pass	2NT
Pass	3NT	End	

West leads ◇6 against your 3NT contract and East produces the jack. Against moderate opposition you should win with the queen, deliberately letting West know that you also hold the king. You cross to a heart and run the jack of clubs to the king. Knowing that you hold the king of diamonds, West may now switch to spades, hoping to give his partner the lead for a diamond through your king. Reprieved from the noose, you will score nine tricks.

The situation is more complex when West is a strong player. When you win the first trick with the diamond queen, he may ask himself 'Why is declarer letting me know that he holds the king? Perhaps it is bare and will drop under the ace.' Against a strong West, a double-bluff of the king might work better.

Play high to tempt a cover, low to deter one

Suppose now that you are declarer in a trump contract and have several trump honours in sequence. In general, you will play the highest honour when you want the defenders to take the trick, the lowest when you do not. Suppose this is the trump suit:

$$\spadesuit \quad 8\ 5\ 4\ 2$$
$$\spadesuit \quad K\ 7 \qquad\qquad \spadesuit \quad A$$
$$\spadesuit \quad Q\ J\ 10\ 9\ 6\ 3$$

If you are broaching the suit from hand, lead the queen. Although it is a clear-cut mistake to do so, there are countless defenders who will leap in with the king, crashing partner's ace. If you lead the 9 or the 3, there is little chance of this happening.

Suppose instead that there is a risk of an adverse ruff and you are hoping to sneak through a round of trumps from this holding:

$$\spadesuit \quad 8\ 5\ 4\ 2$$
$$\spadesuit \quad A\ 9 \qquad\qquad \spadesuit \quad 7\ 3$$
$$\spadesuit \quad K\ Q\ J\ 10\ 6$$

An inexperienced West is most likely to duck if you lead the 10. He will hope that partner can win with a cheaper honour than his ace. Against a stronger West, you might choose the queen. He may fear that you hold Q J 10 7 6 3 and that he will crash his partner's king if he rises with the ace. The card that cannot be right is the king.

Similar considerations may apply in a side suit. On the following deal, declarer wanted his left-hand opponent to play low rather than high when he opened the club suit:

Love all
Dealer South

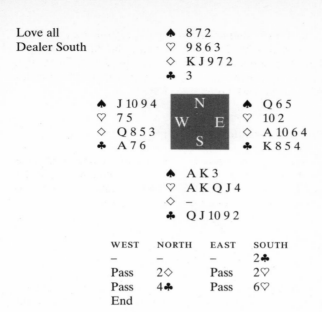

<pre>
        ♠ 8 7 2
        ♡ 9 8 6 3
        ◇ K J 9 7 2
        ♣ 3
♠ J 10 9 4   ♠ Q 6 5
♡ 7 5   ♡ 10 2
◇ Q 8 5 3   ◇ A 10 6 4
♣ A 7 6   ♣ K 8 5 4
        ♠ A K 3
        ♡ A K Q J 4
        ◇ –
        ♣ Q J 10 9 2
</pre>

WEST	NORTH	EAST	SOUTH
–	–	–	2♣
Pass	2◇	Pass	2♡
Pass	4♣	Pass	6♡
End			

North's 4♣ was a splinter bid (see Chapter 10), agreeing hearts as trumps and showing a singleton or void club. West led ♠J and declarer won with the king. He now led a cunning ♣9 from hand. By playing the lowest from equals, he hoped to make it more difficult for West to rise with an honour.

His luck was in. Even though West could see that his ace might be ruffed away later, he was too mean to part with the card on the first round. East won with the club king and cleared the spade suit. After West's duck of the club ace the contract could not be beaten. Declarer led ♣10, covered by the ace and ruffed. He then drew trumps in two rounds and threw dummy's spade loser on his club suit. A spade ruff in dummy brought the total to twelve tricks.

Suppose instead that declarer had led the queen of clubs at trick 2. Even the most dormant of Wests would have risen with the ace. Note also that covering the 9 with the ace would be the winning defence when South held ♣K J 10 9 2.

Disguising that you have a guess to make

When you have a guess to make in a suit, you can sometimes improve your prospects by a judicious choice from equal cards. How would you have played this hand:

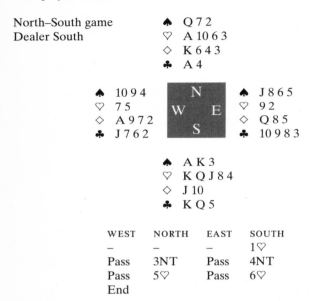

North–South game
Dealer South

♠ Q 7 2
♡ A 10 6 3
◇ K 6 4 3
♣ A 4

♠ 10 9 4
♡ 7 5
◇ A 9 7 2
♣ J 7 6 2

♠ J 8 6 5
♡ 9 2
◇ Q 8 5
♣ 10 9 8 3

♠ A K 3
♡ K Q J 8 4
◇ J 10
♣ K Q 5

WEST	NORTH	EAST	SOUTH
–	–	–	1♡
Pass	3NT	Pass	4NT
Pass	5♡	Pass	6♡
End			

North's 3NT is conventional, indicating a sound raise to game in hearts. You arrive in Six Hearts and win the ♠10 lead with the ace. What now?

To make the slam you will have to guess right in diamonds. Suppose you delay this guess until the final moment. West will know that the defenders need two diamond tricks to beat the slam. There will be no chance at all of his rising with the ace, thereby saving you a guess. The way to apply pressure on West is by leading a diamond at trick 2! If you lead the jack, he is more likely to realise that you have a potential guess in the suit. Place your ◇10 on the table and he will have a very difficult decision to make. What's more he will have only a split second in which to make it. Once he starts to think, it will be clear that he holds the ace.

There is no right or wrong action from West's hand. If your ◇10 is a singleton and you have an unavoidable loser elsewhere, West should take his ace. If ◇10 is from J 10 he must play low smoothly and hope that you misguess the suit. Even the best of defenders will go wrong when you apply pressure in this way.

POINTS TO REMEMBER

1. Defending in the third seat, play the bottom card from equals (for example, the 10 from Q J 10).

2. Defending in the second seat, play the top card from equals (K from K Q J).

3. When winning a trick in fourth position, or in third position under the dummy, capture with the lowest adequate card.

4. When finessing, as declarer, you should generally disguise your holding by playing the top card of equals (finesse the queen, rather than the jack from A Q J).

5. When winning a trick, as declarer, win with the higher card to disguise your strength in a suit (for example, capture the jack with the king from K Q 4). An exception is when you hold the ace and king, playing in no trumps. If you win the queen with the ace the defenders may conclude, from your failure to hold up, that you also hold the king.

6. When you hold several cards in sequence, as declarer, play a high card when you want the defenders to win the trick, a low card when you want them to duck.

TEST YOURSELF

A.

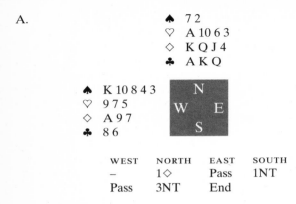

	♠ 7 2
	♡ A 10 6 3
	◇ K Q J 4
	♣ A K Q

♠ K 10 8 4 3
♡ 9 7 5
◇ A 9 7
♣ 8 6

WEST	NORTH	EAST	SOUTH
–	1◇	Pass	1NT
Pass	3NT	End	

You lead ♠4 against 3NT and partner plays the queen, won by South's ace. Declarer now leads ◇10 from his hand. What will you play when you take your ◇A? (If you hold up for a round or two, partner will signal that he holds three diamonds.)

B.

♠ A 7 4
♡ A 8 6
◇ 10 9 2
♣ A K Q J

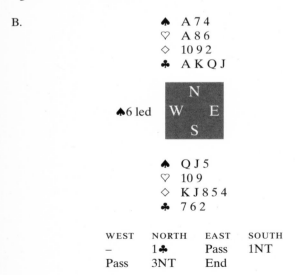

♠6 led

♠ Q J 5
♡ 10 9
◇ K J 8 5 4
♣ 7 6 2

WEST	NORTH	EAST	SOUTH
–	1♣	Pass	1NT
Pass	3NT	End	

West leads ♠6 against 3NT, East playing the 10. Which honour will you use to win the trick? Why did you choose this card?

ANSWERS

A. Partner's queen of spades denies the jack. If South holds such as: ♠A J ♡K 8 2 ◇10 6 3 ♣10 7 5 3 2, the only winning defence is to rise immediately with the diamond ace and lay down the king of spades. This is just one particular hand for South, however, and it is much more likely that his spade holding is A J x. You should look for a way to give partner the lead, so he can play a spade through declarer's jack. The best chance is to switch to a heart. If partner has ♡K, the contract will then go down.

B. You should win the first trick with the queen (playing the higher of touching honours, as declarer). Your plan is to cross to dummy with a club and to run ◇10. If this loses to the queen, a heart switch will surely kill the contract. By winning the first round of spades with the queen rather than the jack, you leave open the possibility (in West's eyes) that East has played ♠10 from a J 10 combination. West may therefore take the losing option of continuing spades. If instead you win the first trick with the spade jack, West can place you with the spade queen and will surely switch to hearts.

8. Support Doubles and Redoubles

The more people play bridge, the more they realise the importance of the total number of trumps held by a partnership. Hardened bridge professionals may relish the idea of playing in a 4-3 fit. Ordinary mortals like us are far happier with a 4-4 or 5-3 fit. When the trump fit is 5-4 or better, hands become very easy to play and yield a surprising number of tricks.

Because the total number of trumps is so critical, several recent changes in bidding theory aim to show precisely how many trumps a player holds. Before we look at one of the most important of these ideas, it will pay us to look closely at a guideline for competitive bidding that has become widely accepted:

The Law of Total Tricks
Even when your side has no advantage in terms of high-card points, you should be willing to compete to the level dictated by your total number of trumps.

So, with eight trumps you should compete to the two-level (contracting for eight tricks). With nine trumps you should compete to the three-level. And so on. If you suffer a penalty in doing so, you will usually find that the opponents could have done better by playing a contract their way.

Way back in Chapter 1 we said it was good tactics to raise a 1♠ overall to 3♠ on a fairly weak hand with 4-card support. This was an example of the Law of Total Tricks in action – with nine trumps between you, compete to the three-level.

On now to the details of a convention that lets you know how many total trumps are held in one common situation. Look at this start to an auction:

WEST	NORTH	EAST	SOUTH
1♢	Pass	1♠	2♡
2♠			

Playing traditional methods, West will sometimes make such a raise with only three spades. East may find the subsequent auction difficult to judge, particularly if he has only four spades himself. Unwilling to accept this inaccuracy, many tournament players follow this scheme after the fourth-seat overcall:

- with 4-card support for responder, make a limit bid,
- with 3-card support, double.

The conventional double, to show 3-card support, is known as a Support Double. Here is an example of such a call:

West	North	East	South	WEST
1♢	Pass	1♠	2♡	♠ J 9 6
Dble				♡ A 7
				♢ A Q 8 5 4 3
				♣ Q 5

West doubles, to show his 3-card spade support. The bid says nothing at all about the strength of his hand. He may hold 11 points, he may hold 20 points. When responder makes his next bid, he will assume for the moment a minimum hand opposite. The opener will indicate any surplus strength on the next round.

Let's see a graphic example of the difference between 4-card support and 3-card support.

Love all
Dealer South

```
                    ♠ K 8 5 4 2
                    ♡ 9 5 4
                    ♢ 10 7
                    ♣ A 8 2

    ♠ Q 7              N           ♠ J 9
    ♡ 10 6 2                       ♡ A K Q 8 3
    ♢ A 8 6       W       E        ♢ 9 5 2
    ♣ Q 10 7 6 4      S            ♣ K J 3

                    ♠ A 10 6 3
                    ♡ J 7
                    ♢ K Q J 4 3
                    ♣ 9 5
```

WEST	NORTH	EAST	SOUTH
–	–	–	1♢
Pass	1♠	2♡	2♠ (1)
3♡	3♠	End	

(1) shows 4-card spade support

Sitting North, playing Support Doubles, you know from partner's direct raise that there are nine trumps between the two hands. Following the Law of Total Tricks, you should be willing to compete to 3♠.

Here the cards lie favourably for you and the contract will be made. Suppose that West held ♠Q J 9, however, and 3♠ went one down. It would be in a good cause. East–West would have one fewer loser in their heart contract (since East would hold a singleton spade). Their contract of 3♡ would surely have succeeded and −50 would therefore be a good result for you.

Suppose now that South holds only 3-card spade support:

Love all
Dealer South

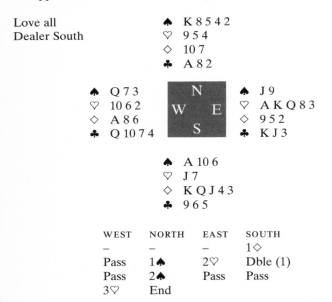

```
                    ♠  K 8 5 4 2
                    ♡  9 5 4
                    ◇  10 7
                    ♣  A 8 2

    ♠  Q 7 3                         ♠  J 9
    ♡  10 6 2          N             ♡  A K Q 8 3
    ◇  A 8 6        W     E          ◇  9 5 2
    ♣  Q 10 7 4        S             ♣  K J 3

                    ♠  A 10 6
                    ♡  J 7
                    ◇  K Q J 4 3
                    ♣  9 6 5
```

WEST	NORTH	EAST	SOUTH
–	–	–	1◇
Pass	1♠	2♡	Dble (1)
Pass	2♠	Pass	Pass
3♡	End		

(1) Support Double, showing 3-card spade support.

Look first at the North–South cards. What a difference it makes, with South holding only three trumps! First of all, there is now a loser in the trump suit despite the favourable break. Secondly, South has one more club, introducing a second loser in that suit. North–South have eight trumps between them. The Law suggests that they should compete to the 2♠ level. So they should. The contract will go one down but that's all right because 2♡ would have succeeded.

Now look at the East–West cards. Many West players would take the push to 3♡, as shown here, but it's not the winning action. The contract goes one down and 2♠ would have failed too. East–West hold only eight trumps (not that West knows this) and the Law comes up with the right answer again. They should not compete beyond the 8-trick level.

You may be suspicious of accepting a general conclusion from these two sample lay-outs. If so, test out the Law of Total Tricks on the next few competitive deals you play. You will be surprised how accurate it is.

Auctions involving a Support Double

Let's look at some complete auctions featuring the Support Double.

WEST	EAST	West	North	East	South
♠ A 9 8	♠ Q 7 6 2	1◇	Pass	1♠	2♣
♡ Q 10 8 5	♡ J 4	Dble	Pass	2◇	End
◇ A Q 9 7 5	◇ 10 8 2				
♣ 5	♣ K J 9 3				

If West were not playing Support Doubles, he would no doubt have bid 2♠ at his second turn – not a comfortable spot. As it is, he can use a double to show his 3-card spade support. East has only four spades, so seeks shelter in 2◇.

When the two hands are somewhat stronger, the bidding may continue along natural lines:

WEST	EAST	West	North	East	South
♠ A 9 8	♠ K 7 6 2	1◇	Pass	1♠	2♣
♡ K 10 8 5	♡ A 4	Dble	Pass	2NT	Pass
◇ A Q 9 7 5	◇ 10 8 2	3NT	End		
♣ 5	♣ K J 9 3				

East's 2NT is natural, showing a stopper or two in clubs. It suggests also that the spade fit is only 4-3. Here West has enough to raise to game.

A second-round return to the opener's suit passes the same message:

		West	North	East	South
WEST	EAST	1♣	Pass	1♠	2♡
♠ K 6 2	♠ A 9 7 3	Dble	Pass	3♣	Pass
♡ A 5 3	♡ Q 7	3♡	Pass	3NT	End
◇ J 6	◇ K 10 2				
♣ A K Q 7 3	♣ J 9 4 2				

East shows support for partner's clubs, implying that he holds only four spades. West can see advantage in making East declarer in no-trumps, should he hold such as ♡Q x or ♡J x x. He shows his strength with a cue-bid of 3♡ and East duly bids 3NT on his half-stop. Played by East, the contract is an excellent one.

When responder does hold five or more trumps, the bidding will again continue along natural lines:

		West	North	East	South
WEST	EAST	1◇	Pass	1♠	2♡
♠ Q 6 2	♠ K J 10 7 3	Dble	Pass	3♠	Pass
♡ A 5	♡ J 7 2	4♠	End		
◇ A 6 4	◇ Q 8 2				
♣ K Q 7 6 4	♣ A 3				

East is happy to make spades trumps and is strong enough to invite game. West, with a well-disposed 15 points, accepts the invitation.

When partner does not make a Support Double

What do you make of this auction (when Support Doubles are being played)?

West	North	East	South		EAST
1◇	Pass	1♠	2♡		♠ Q 9 7 6 2
Pass	Pass	?			♡ J 4 3
					◇ 10 8
					♣ A J 9

West has denied three spades! This tilts the odds well against competing, either with 2♠ or a take-out double. Pass, and lead ◇10, hoping to beat the heart contract.

The same is true when the opener rebids elsewhere:

West	North	East	South		EAST
1◇	Pass	1♠	2♣	♠	K 10 8 6 4 2
2◇	Pass	?		♡	K 4 3
				◇	6 2
				♣	J 9

Again West has denied three spades. With only five diamonds, West might have passed at his second turn. The odds are high that West has six diamonds. Since he cannot hold more than two spades, there is no reason to think that a spade contract will play better than one in diamonds. You should pass.

How high do Support Doubles apply?

A double by the opener is a Support Double if he had the opportunity to give a single raise of responder's suit. When the defender in the fourth seat makes a jump overcall, a double by the opener shows general strength instead. It is for take-out and does not carry a message of 3-card support. Look at this auction:

West	North	East	South		WEST
1◇	Pass	1♠	3♣	♠	Q 9 7
?				♡	A 4
				◇	K J 8 6 5 2
				♣	Q 6

The bidding has been pushed beyond the safety barrier of 2♠. It would not be sound now to double on all hands with 3-card spade support. If East held only four spades and a 6-count, a double might carry the partnership too high. Here West should pass. If partner keeps the bidding alive with a take-out double, the spade support can be shown then.

The Support Redouble

Suppose the bidding starts in the same way (1◇ – Pass – 1♠) and the defender on your right makes a take-out double. A redouble by you will now show 3-card support for partner:

West	North	East	South		WEST
1◇	Pass	1♠	Dble	♠	Q 9 7
Rdble				♡	4
				◇	A K 8 6 2
				♣	A 9 7 3

The bidding will continue along exactly the same lines that flow from a Support Double. The inferences when partner does not make a Support Redouble are the same, too. Any direct raise in spades would again promise 4-card support.

POINTS TO REMEMBER

1. Even when your side is outgunned in terms of points, it will generally be right to compete to the level dictated by your total trump length. With eight trumps between the hands, you will compete to the two-level; with nine trumps, to the three-level.

2. When the opener has the opportunity to give a single raise of responder's suit, but chooses instead to double an overcall on his right, this is a **Support Double**. It shows 3-card support for responder's suit.

3. When the opener spurns a Support Double and raises partner directly, to any level, this shows at least 4-card support.

4. When the opener has the opportunity to make a Support Double, but chooses instead to pass or make any rebid other than a raise, he denies 3-card support for responder.

5. When the player to opener's right has made a take-out double (in an auction such as 1◇ – Pass – 1♡ – Dble), the opener may make a Support Redouble. Again, this shows 3-card support for responder.

TEST YOURSELF

What would you bid on the following hands? The vulnerability is not important but you may assume that it is Love All.

A.

West	North	East	South	WEST
1♣	Pass	1♡	2♢	♠ A 7
?				♡ 10 4 2
				♢ A 2
				♣ A K J 9 7 2

B.

West	North	East	South	WEST
1♢	Pass	1♡	2♠	♠ 7 4
?				♡ K 6 5
				♢ A J 8 7 6 2
				♣ A 5

C.

West	North	East	South	EAST
1♢	Pass	1♠	2♣	♠ A 9 7 3
Dble	Pass	?		♡ 9 6 5
				♢ J 5 2
				♣ A 10 7

D.

West	North	East	South	EAST
1♢	Pass	1♠	2♣	♠ K 9 7 3 2
Dble	3♣	?		♡ A 7 4
				♢ 9 2
				♣ J 10 5

E.

West	North	East	South	WEST
1♢	Pass	1♠	Dble	♠ K 7 4
?				♡ K 6
				♢ A K 10 9 7 6
				♣ A 5

ANSWERS

A. Double. Despite your good clubs, your first duty is to make a Support Double, showing 3-card support for partner's hearts.

B. Pass. Here the level is too high for a Support Double. You are not strong enough to bid 3◇, so for the moment you must pass.

C. 2◇. The spade fit is only 4-3. To indicate this, you should mark time with 2◇. Add another point or two and you would rebid 2NT, again implying that you held only four spades.

D. Pass. It may seem tempting to compete with 3♠ but there are only eight trumps between the hands. Since you have no clear balance of the points, unless partner chooses to bid again, the Law of Total Tricks suggests you should not compete beyond the two-level. Facing a direct raise to 2♠ instead, you would have competed to the three-level.

E. Redouble. You make a Support Redouble, to show the 3-card spade support. If partner signs off in 2♠ you will bid 3◇ to show your extra strength and good diamond suit.

9. Ace for Attitude, King for Count

Which card do you normally lead from an ace-king combination, the ace or the king? For decades the card led was merely a matter of fashion. It made no difference which style of lead you preferred, so long as partner knew.

A recent innovation is to vary your lead from ace-king, according to the type of signal you would like partner to make. This is the scheme:

- Lead the **ace** when you require an **attitude** signal.
- Lead the **king** when you require a **count** signal.

(An attitude signal, remember, is where you play high to encourage, low to discourage. A count signal is where you play high with an even number of cards, low with an odd number.)

You have a similar choice when leading from a king-queen combination. Partner will signal his count on a king lead, as we have said. He will give an attitude signal if you lead the queen:

- Lead the **queen** when you require an **attitude** signal.

Perhaps you don't think it will be easy to know which type of signal you want on a particular hand. We will look straight away at some sample deals, to see the two different types of signal in operation.

Ace for Attitude

When you are defending a suit contract up to the level of Four Spades, it is usually a poor idea to lead the ace of a side suit, unless you also hold the king. When your holding is relatively short (A K x or A K x x) you will normally lead the ace from ace-king. The message will be: I have the ace-king of this suit; please play high if you would like me to continue the suit.

This is a typical deal:

Love all   ♠ Q J 7 5
Dealer South   ♡ 8 6 5
                   ◇ Q 7
                   ♣ A Q J 4

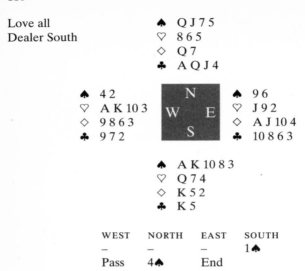

♠ 4 2   ♠ 9 6
♡ A K 10 3   ♡ J 9 2
◇ 9 8 6 3   ◇ A J 10 4
♣ 9 7 2   ♣ 10 8 6 3

♠ A K 10 8 3
♡ Q 7 4
◇ K 5 2
♣ K 5

WEST	NORTH	EAST	SOUTH
–	–	–	1♠
Pass	4♠	End	

West leads the ace of hearts, requesting an attitude signal. East discourages with the 2 and West now switches to ◇9, declarer playing low from dummy. If East allows the 9 to run to South's king, there is an evident risk that declarer will be able to draw trumps and take some discards on dummy's clubs. East therefore rises with the ace of diamonds and fires back a heart, putting the contract one down.

King for Count

The situation is different when the contract is at the five-level or higher, or when the leader holds five or more cards to the ace-king. In both these cases it is unlikely that the third round of the side suit will be of consequence (declarer will usually be ruffing in one hand or the other). What the defender on lead needs to know is whether a second round of his suit will stand up. He therefore leads the king, requesting a count signal.

Suppose you are West on this deal:

East–West game
Dealer South

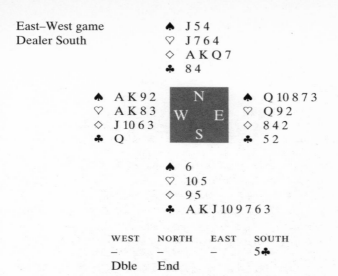

```
                      ♠ J 5 4
                      ♡ J 7 6 4
                      ◇ A K Q 7
                      ♣ 8 4
♠ A K 9 2          N          ♠ Q 10 8 7 3
♡ A K 8 3      W       E      ♡ Q 9 2
◇ J 10 6 3         S          ◇ 8 4 2
♣ Q                          ♣ 5 2
                      ♠ 6
                      ♡ 10 5
                      ◇ 9 5
                      ♣ A K J 10 9 7 6 3
```

WEST	NORTH	EAST	SOUTH
–	–	–	5♣
Dble	End		

South opens with a pre-emptive bid of 5♣ and you double on the West cards. Using 'ace for attitude, king for count', you will lead one of the kings. Let's say that you lead the king of spades. When dummy appears, it is clear that you will need to cash three winners in the majors. East has been requested to give a count signal. With five spades, an odd number, he signals with his lowest spot-card, the 3.

You now know that it will be dangerous to play the ace of spades next. If East holds five spades (rather than three), declarer will ruff, draw trumps, and no doubt make the contract. So, you lead the king of hearts next, again requesting a count signal. East signals with the 2 and South follows suit. South must hold another heart! If not, East would have started with four hearts and would have signalled high. You therefore continue with the ace of hearts, defeating the contract.

Suppose you weren't playing this method and had no way to ask for a count signal. After cashing one trick in each major, you would have to guess what to do next. Since dummy is slightly shorter in spades, you might try to cash a second spade. Disaster!

You would lead the king from ace-king against a slam contract, too. On the next deal your continuation depends on the count signal that partner makes.

Game all   ♠ K 10 4
Dealer North   ♡ K Q 6
                  ◇ Q 7 3
                  ♣ K 10 8 4

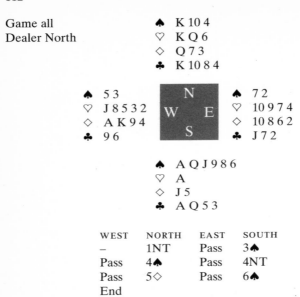

    ♠ 5 3   ♠ 7 2
    ♡ J 8 5 3 2   N   ♡ 10 9 7 4
    ◇ A K 9 4   W   E   ◇ 10 8 6 2
    ♣ 9 6   S   ♣ J 7 2

                  ♠ A Q J 9 8 6
                  ♡ A
                  ◇ J 5
                  ♣ A Q 5 3

WEST	NORTH	EAST	SOUTH
–	1NT	Pass	3♠
Pass	4♠	Pass	4NT
Pass	5◇	Pass	6♠
End			

North opens a 12–14 point 1NT and admits to one key card (♠K) in response to Roman Key-Card Blackwood. Sitting West, you lead the king of diamonds against the spade slam, declarer following with a deceptive jack. Should you try to cash a second diamond?

Forget about South's jack of diamonds! The card you want to see is partner's length signal. Here he will play the 8, to show an even number of cards. (As we saw in Chapter 4, it is normal to signal with the second best card from four.) You know now that a second diamond will stand up. You cash the ace of diamonds and the slam is one down. Any other continuation and declarer would throw his remaining diamond loser on the hearts.

Let's alter the South hand, giving him only one diamond:

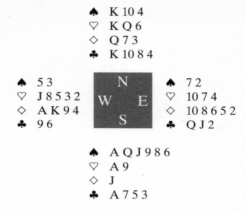

```
                    ♠  K 10 4
                    ♡  K Q 6
                    ◇  Q 7 3
                    ♣  K 10 8 4
     ♠  5 3            N          ♠  7 2
     ♡  J 8 5 3 2                 ♡  10 7 4
     ◇  A K 9 4    W      E       ◇  10 8 6 5 2
     ♣  9 6            S          ♣  Q J 2
                    ♠  A Q J 9 8 6
                    ♡  A 9
                    ◇  J
                    ♣  A 7 5 3
```

Again you lead ◇K, the jack appearing from South. Now it would be fatal to continue with the diamond ace. You would set up the dummy's queen for a second club discard. You will now have a different count signal from partner, however. He will play the 2, showing an odd number of diamonds. The risk of trying to cash a second diamond would be apparent and you would be well advised to switch elsewhere at trick two. Declarer would then have an unavoidable loser in clubs. One down!

The king lead at no-trumps

Against a no-trump contract, the lead of a king implies a strong holding in the suit. It asks partner to unblock any honour card that he may hold, to give a count signal otherwise.

Let's look at a few single-suit positions.

```
                ♡  7 6 3
    ♡  A K J 10 5           ♡  9 8 2
                ♡  Q 4
```

You lead ♡K against 3NT and partner plays the 2. What deductions can you make? Partner does not hold the queen (or he would have played it under your king). His 2 shows that he has either one heart or three. Often the bidding will have ruled out the possibility that South has four hearts to partner's one. You will continue with the ace of hearts, dropping South's queen.

Here the position is less favourable:

$$\heartsuit \quad 7\ 6\ 3$$

$$\heartsuit \quad A\ K\ J\ 10\ 5 \qquad \qquad \heartsuit \quad 8\ 2$$

$$\heartsuit \quad Q\ 9\ 4$$

You lead $\heartsuit$K again and declarer drops the 9, hoping to look like a man with $\heartsuit$Q 9. The ruse may fool some people, but not you or me! Partner's 8 denies the queen and shows an even number of cards. So, declarer's queen must still be guarded. Unless you have a certain card of entry, and are happy to concede a heart trick, you must switch elsewhere. You hope to put partner on lead to play through South's queen.

You would lead the king also from a powerful holding headed by the king-queen:

$$\diamondsuit \quad A\ 8\ 4$$

$$\diamondsuit \quad K\ Q\ 10\ 9\ 5 \qquad \qquad \diamondsuit \quad 7\ 6\ 3$$

$$\diamondsuit \quad J\ 2$$

You lead $\diamondsuit$K against 3NT, drawing the 4, 3 and 2. Can you read the lie of the cards? Partner has denied the diamond jack (he would have unblocked it). He has also shown an odd number of cards in the suit. If this is three, rather than one, declarer's jack will fall under your queen. Continuing with the queen is attractive, particularly if the bidding allows you to rule out a 4-card diamond holding with South.

The situation would be different if your partner had played the 7 or the 6 at trick 1. Placing him with a doubleton (or singleton) diamond, you would know that a diamond continuation would cost a trick.

Ace leads against high-level contracts

We have already seen that it is standard to lead the king from ace-king against contracts at the five-level or higher. It follows that when you lead an ace against such a contract you will not hold the king. Partner should encourage only when he himself holds the king.

Game all   ♠ A K Q J 4
Dealer North   ♡ Q J 9 4
        ◇ J 6
        ♣ A 5

  ♠ 7 3 2   ♠ 10 9 8 5
  ♡ 10 8 7 2   ♡ A 6 5
  ◇ A 7 5 4   ◇ Q 10 9 2
  ♣ 8 7   ♣ K 4

       ♠ 6
       ♡ K 3
       ◇ K 8 3
       ♣ Q J 10 9 6 3 2

WEST	NORTH	EAST	SOUTH
–	1♠	Pass	2♣
Pass	2♡	Pass	3♣
Pass	4♣	Pass	5♣
End			

When North–South reach 5♣, having bid all the suits except diamonds, West is entitled to place the ace of diamonds on the table. This card asks for an attitude signal. Since the contract is at the five-level (or higher), East must signal his attitude on the assumption that partner holds the ace but not the king. He duly signals with the 2, telling West that he does not hold the diamond king.

No further tricks will come from the diamond suit (or the spade suit, of course) and West duly switches to hearts. East pockets a trick with the heart ace and his trump king beats the contract in due course. You can see what would happen if West played another diamond at trick 2. Declarer would win with the king, ruff a diamond, then play the ace of trumps and turn to the spade suit. His heart loser would vanish into the night and the contract would be made.

Queen for Attitude

The lead of a queen requests an attitude signal, whether the contract is in no-trumps or not. Such a lead may be made from a combination headed by the queen-jack, or from one headed by the king-queen when you would prefer an attitude signal to a count signal. Partner will encourage when holding the ace, king or jack.

Suppose you are West here:

```
              ◇  6 4
◇  K Q 10 5              ◇  A 8 3
              ◇  J 9 7 2
```

A count signal would be of little use. If your king won the trick you would have no idea whether to play a second round. You should lead the queen, requesting an attitude signal. Since partner holds an honour, he will encourage with the 8. You continue with ◇5 to the ace and score four tricks in the suit.

Here the layout is less friendly:

```
              ◇  6 4
◇  K Q 10 5              ◇  9 8 7 3
              ◇  A J 2
```

Your queen draws the 4, 3 and 2. Since partner has discouraged, you know that declarer is lying in wait with the ace-jack (a Bath Coup). You will switch elsewhere.

When declarer has four cards to the ace-jack, he can make life more difficult for you:

```
              ◇  6 4
◇  K Q 10 5              ◇  9 7 3
              ◇  A J 8 2
```

You lead ◇Q, drawing the 4, 3 and a cunning 8 from declarer. Declarer has false-carded in the hope that you will read partner's ◇3 as an encouraging card from A 3 2 or J 3 2. The odds are high that the cards lie as in the diagram. You should ask yourself: where is the 7? If partner does hold such as J 3 2, declarer has played the 8 from A 9 8 7. Few declarers are as clever as that!

Occasionally, against a no-trump contract, you would lead 'queen for attitude' from an A K Q combination:

```
              ♠  7 6
♠  A K Q 2              ♠  J 8 4
              ♠  10 9 5 3
```

When you lead the queen, East encourages with the 8. You continue with the 2 and bring in the suit. The king would be the wrong card to lead. Partner would unblock the jack, as requested, and declarer would then score a trick in the suit.

POINTS TO REMEMBER

1. Against both suit and no-trump contracts, you should lead the ace from ace-king to request an attitude signal. The lead of a king requests a count signal (or, in no-trump contracts only, to unblock an honour).

2. Against suit contracts up to the level of 4♠ the attitude signal to an ace is based on the assumption that the lead is from an AK combination. Against higher suit contracts, the signaller assumes the lead is from the ace (from a holding headed by the ace-king, the king would have been led).

3. The lead of a queen also asks for an attitude signal. You would lead the queen from sequences headed by the queen (such as Q J 10 4 or Q J 9 8 3) also from lesser holdings headed by the king-queen (K Q 10 3 or K Q 2).

TEST YOURSELF

A.

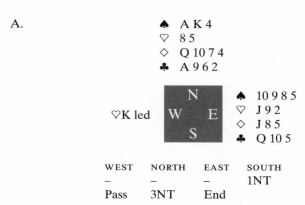

```
              ♠  A K 4
              ♡  8 5
              ◇  Q 10 7 4
              ♣  A 9 6 2

                    N            ♠  10 9 8 5
      ♡K led    W       E        ♡  J 9 2
                    S            ◇  J 8 5
                                 ♣  Q 10 5
```

WEST	NORTH	EAST	SOUTH
–	–	–	1NT
Pass	3NT	End	

Partner leads ♡K against South's 3NT. What card will you play? Suppose South had opened 1♠ instead and was now playing in 4♠. Would that make any difference to the card you chose to play?

B.

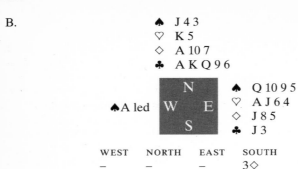

```
                        ♠  J 4 3
                        ♡  K 5
                        ◇  A 10 7
                        ♣  A K Q 9 6
                                        ♠  Q 10 9 5
                    N                   ♡  A J 6 4
        ♠A led    W     E               ◇  J 8 5
                    S                   ♣  J 3
```

WEST	NORTH	EAST	SOUTH
–	–	–	3◇
Pass	5◇	End	

Partner leads ♠A. Which card will you play to this trick?

C.

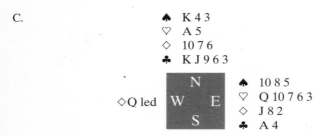

```
                        ♠  K 4 3
                        ♡  A 5
                        ◇  10 7 6
                        ♣  K J 9 6 3
                                        ♠  10 8 5
                    N                   ♡  Q 10 7 6 3
        ◇Q led    W     E               ◇  J 8 2
                    S                   ♣  A 4
```

South and North bid 1♠ – 2♣, 2♠ – 4♠. Your partner then leads ◇Q.
What sort of holding will he have? Which card will you play on the first
trick?

D.

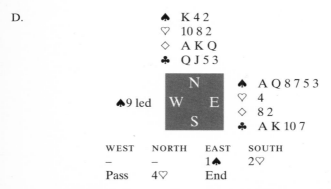

```
                        ♠  K 4 2
                        ♡  10 8 2
                        ◇  A K Q
                        ♣  Q J 5 3
                                        ♠  A Q 8 7 5 3
                    N                   ♡  4
        ♠9 led    W     E               ◇  8 2
                    S                   ♣  A K 10 7
```

WEST	NORTH	EAST	SOUTH
–	–	1♠	2♡
Pass	4♡	End	

Partner leads ♠9 against the South's heart game. You win with the
queen and declarer plays the 10. How will you defend?

ANSWERS

A. Against a no-trump contract, a king lead asks for 'unblock or count'. You should therefore unblock the jack. Partner will have a strong holding such as K Q 10 9 3. When he sees your jack, he will know that it is safe to continue the suit. If the contract were 4♠ instead, you would give a count signal. Here you would play the 2.

B. Against a five-level contract partner would have led the king from ace-king, to ask for count. His ♠A lead, presumably not backed by the king, asks for an attitude signal. Since you do not hold the king, you should discourage with the 5. Partner will switch to hearts and you may score two tricks there.

C. Partner has a diamond sequence headed by the king-queen. (The only other possibility, a doubleton or singleton queen, is precluded by the bidding.) A queen lead requests an attitude signal. Since you hold the jack, you will encourage with the 8. If declarer holds up the ace, partner will know that it is safe to continue the suit.

D. Knowing that two rounds of spades will stand up (partner would not lead the 9 from J 9 6), you should cash the spade ace at trick 2. If partner shows out on the second round, give him a spade ruff, leading a low spade for the ruff, so he will be sure to return a club. If instead partner follows to the second spade, continue with the king of clubs requesting a count signal. A low card from partner will tell you that a second club will stand up. If partner plays high, and his spot-card is consistent with a second-best signal from four cards, it is best to continue with a third round of spades. This will promote a trump trick for partner if he holds Q x or J x x in the trump suit.

10. Fit Jumps and Splinter Bids

A limit raise, such as 1♠ – 2♠ or 1♡ – 3♡, gives a fair picture of responder's general strength. It ignores one important factor, though: do the side suits fit together well?

Look at these two hands:

WEST	EAST
♠ 9 5	♠ J 3
♡ A Q J 10 8 3	♡ K 9 6 2
◇ A 10 3 2	◇ 9 7 5
♣ 2	♣ K Q J 7

The black suits fit poorly, with East's club strength wasted opposite a singleton. If you reached 4♡ and the defenders attacked diamonds early on, you would probably go two down – losing two spades, two diamonds and a club.

See what happens if we switch East's minor suits:

WEST	EAST
♠ 9 5	♠ J 3
♡ A Q J 10 8 3	♡ K 9 6 2
◇ A 10 3 2	◇ K Q J 7
♣ 2	♣ 9 7 5

The hands now fit excellently. East's diamond strength pulls its full weight, facing length in the other hand, and game in hearts will be easy.

Wouldn't it be great if there was a way to raise partner's suit and at the same time show your main side suit? In several situations, there is! You can use bids known as 'fit jumps'.

Fit jumps after an opposing double

When your partner's opening bid has been doubled for take-out, there is little point in the traditional (slam invitational) meaning of a jump shift. Instead you should use such a jump to show a fit for partner with a good side suit. The minimum strength of the hand will be that of a sound raise to the three-level.

This deal includes the two hands we saw a moment ago:

Love all
Dealer West

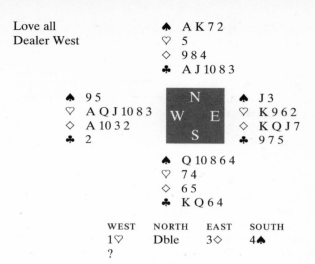

♠ A K 7 2
♡ 5
◇ 9 8 4
♣ A J 10 8 3

♠ 9 5
♡ A Q J 10 8 3
◇ A 10 3 2
♣ 2

♠ J 3
♡ K 9 6 2
◇ K Q J 7
♣ 9 7 5

♠ Q 10 8 6 4
♡ 7 4
◇ 6 5
♣ K Q 6 4

WEST	NORTH	EAST	SOUTH
1♡	Dble	3◇	4♠
?			

East's 3◇ is a fit jump, showing a raise to 3♡ (at least) with a good diamond side suit. You see what a strong position West is now in? He knows that his side has a double fit in the red suits and therefore that the opponents have a double fit in the black suits. He can hardly lose by bidding to the Five level. Here the sacrifice in 5♡ will go only one down and 4♠ is cold the other way.

Now let's switch East's minors. This might be the lay-out:

Love all
Dealer West

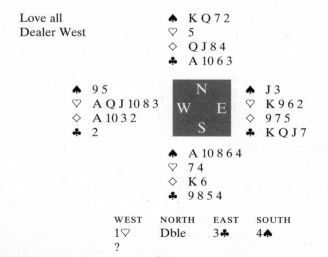

♠ K Q 7 2
♡ 5
◇ Q J 8 4
♣ A 10 6 3

♠ 9 5
♡ A Q J 10 8 3
◇ A 10 3 2
♣ 2

♠ J 3
♡ K 9 6 2
◇ 9 7 5
♣ K Q J 7

♠ A 10 8 6 4
♡ 7 4
◇ K 6
♣ 9 8 5 4

WEST	NORTH	EAST	SOUTH
1♡	Dble	3♣	4♠
?			

Now Four Spades will go down and a sacrifice in Five Hearts may cost 500. Thanks to the use of the fit jump, West is in a good position to judge this. With a singleton facing partner's main side suit, he knows that the East–West hands will fit poorly.

Fit jumps after an opposing overcall

Exactly the same method can be used when your partner's opening bid has been overcalled.

WEST	EAST	West	North	East	South
♠ A K 9 8 3	♠ Q 7 6 2	1♠	2♣	3♡	Pass
♡ Q 8 5	♡ A J 10 6 2	4♠	All Pass		
◇ A 8 4	◇ 9 3				
♣ 10 7	♣ J 3				

West has little more than a minimum but, knowing of a fair heart suit opposite, he tries his luck in game. As it happens, the game depends on a king finesse through the overcaller.

Fit jumps opposite partner's overcall

You may also use a fit jump when your partner has overcalled

WEST	West	North	East	South
♠ 8 7	–	1♠	2♡	2♠
♡ K 10 9 7	?			
◇ A K 7 6 2				
♣ 5 3				

You bid 4◇, showing a raise to 4♡ with a diamond side suit. As before, this call will help partner to judge how well the two hands fit, and therefore how high he should compete. A second benefit is apparent here. If the opponents win the auction, partner will have a good idea of which suit to lead!

High-level fit bids

Sometimes the opponents will remove your bidding space, preventing you from making a fit jump. Nevertheless, logic may dictate that your high-level bid in a new suit cannot be natural or you would have spoken earlier. Your bid will then indicate a fit for partner.

What do you make of West's 4♣ here, for example:

WEST	NORTH	EAST	SOUTH
–	–	–	1♢
Pass	1♡	1♠	3♡
4♣			

It is barely possible that West can have a good enough club suit to justify a natural bid at the four-level. He would surely have spoken on the first round with such a hand. He is showing a spade fit and a club side suit. His aim may be two-fold: to help partner to judge whether to sacrifice over 4♡, and to suggest a good lead if the opponents win the auction.

You may think that there will be occasional auctions where it is not entirely clear whether partner is showing a fit or not. You're right! This is dangerous territory and there have been one or two spectacular misunderstandings, even at world championship level. Even so, the overall advantage flowing from such bids is considerable.

Splinter bids

Perhaps you are already familiar with the different type of fit-showing bid, known as the 'splinter bid'. This is a double jump response in a new suit, such as 1♠ – 4♣. Here the response of 4♣ shows a sound raise to game in spades and a *shortage* in clubs, either a singleton or a void. The aim is the same as that for a fit jump: to allow partner to judge whether the two hands fit well.

West	North	East	South		WEST		EAST
1♠	Pass	4♣	Pass	♠	A Q J 8 4 2	♠	K 10 7 3
4NT	Pass	5♣	Pass	♡	K 7	♡	A 9 6 2
6♠	End			◇	K 3	◇	A 8 6 5
				♣	J 9 3	♣	5

East responds 4♣, showing a game raise in spades that includes at most one club. West can see that the hands fit excellently; he will be able to ruff two club losers. Roman Key-Card Blackwood reveals that East has three key cards (♠K, ♡A, ◇A) and the slam is reached.

Suppose that East's singleton had not been in clubs on that last hand:

West	North	East	South		WEST		EAST
1♠	Pass	4◇	Pass	♠	A Q J 8 4 2	♠	K 10 7 3
4♠	End			♡	K 7	♡	A 9 6 2
				◇	K 3	◇	5
				♣	J 9 3	♣	A 8 6 5

Since a singleton is of little use opposite a king, West knows that the hands fit poorly. He signs off in 4♠ and ten tricks may well be the limit of the hand.

The opener may make a splinter bid too:

West	North	East	South		WEST		EAST
1♡	Pass	1♠	Pass	♠	K J 8 5	♠	A Q 10 9 2
4♣	Pass	4♠	End	♡	A K J 6 2	♡	8 4
				◇	A 8 4	◇	10 9 7
				♣	3	♣	K J 5

East has excellent trumps, but he knows that the hands do not fit well. He signs off and indeed the slam is not a good one . Switch East's minors and the situation would be very different. With a known singleton opposite his ♣10 9 7, the fit could hardly be better. East would head for a slam via Roman Key-Card Blackwood.

As you see from these examples, splinter bids may be used in uncontested auctions. Fit jumps are available only in contested auctions.

Fit jump or splinter?

Which is the better method? Fit jumps (which show a good side suit) or splinter bids (which show a shortage)? In most situations where a fit jump applies, there is no need to choose between them. The two methods can live alongside. A single jump will be a fit-showing bid, a double jump will be a splinter.

West	North	East	South		EAST
1♠	2♣	?		♠	A 9 7 3
				♡	J 4
				◇	K J 9 7 3
				♣	9 3

Here East bids 3◇, a fit jump to show a sound raise to 3♠ (at least) with a diamond side suit.

West	North	East	South		EAST
1♠	2♣	?		♠	K J 8 3
				♡	Q 9 7 6 3
				◇	3
				♣	A 10 5

Now East prefers a (double-jump) splinter bid of 4◇. Partner is more likely to be interested in the singleton diamond than the moderate hearts.

Sometimes the opponent's overcall does not leave enough space for both types of response:

West	North	East	South		EAST
1♠	2♡	?		♠	K Q 8 3
				♡	9 7
				◇	J 3
				♣	A Q 8 4 2

East bids 4♣. Since this is only a single jump, it is a fit jump rather than a splinter bid. If you held the other type of hand, with a singleton club, you would have to start with a cue-bid of 3♡, showing at least a sound raise to 3♠.

POINTS TO REMEMBER

1. A limit raise (such as 1♠ – 3♠) describes the overall strength of your hand, but it does not help partner to assess whether the hands fit well.

2. A 'fit jump' shows a sound raise of partner's suit, plus a good side suit. You can make such a bid in these situations:

- facing an overcall
- when partner's opening bid has been doubled
- when partner's opening bid has been overcalled.

3. A 'splinter bid' is a double jump in a new suit. It shows a sound raise of partner's suit that includes a named singleton or void. For example, the sequence 1♡ – 4◇ shows a sound game raise that includes at most one diamond.

4. In situations where a fit jump may be made, a single jump is a fit jump, a double jump is a splinter bid.

TEST YOURSELF

A.

West	North	East	South	EAST
1♠	2◇	?		♠ A 9 7 3
				♡ K Q 7 6 2
				◇ 8 6
				♣ J 2

What should you respond?

B.

West	North	East	South	EAST
1♡	Dble	?		♠ A J 7
				♡ K 7 6 2
				◇ 9 5
				♣ Q 10 8 3

What should you respond?

C.

	West	North	East	South	EAST
	1♠	Pass	?		♠ K J 7 3
					♡ 10 4
					◇ 8 3
					♣ A J 8 7 2

What should you respond?

D.

	West	North	East	South	EAST
	1♡	Pass	?		♠ K 10 7
					♡ A J 6 2
					◇ 5
					♣ K 10 8 5 3

What should you respond?

E.

	West	North	East	South	EAST
	–	–	–	1♠	♠ 6 2
	2♡	2♠	?		♡ Q J 5 2
					◇ A K 10 7 6
					♣ J 4

How should you respond to partner's overcall?

F.

	West	North	East	South	EAST
	–	–	Pass	1♠	♠ 6
	2◇	3♠	?		♡ J 5 2
					◇ K 10 7 6
					♣ K Q 10 9 7

What will you say now, if anything?

ANSWERS

A. You should make a fit jump response of 3♡. This shows that you are worth a raise to 3♠ (at least) and have a good side suit in hearts.

B. With no side suit worthy of a fit jump, you should make the traditional response of 2NT. This shows a sound raise to 3♡ (at least) without a good side suit.

C. Remember that fit jumps facing an opening bid do not apply unless a defender has overcalled or doubled. Here 3♣ would be a standard (very strong) jump shift. You should respond with a limit bid of 3♠.

D. You should make the double-jump response of 4◇, a splinter bid. This will tell partner that you have a sound raise to game, including at most one diamond.

E. You should make a single-jump response of 4◇, showing a sound raise to game and a diamond side suit. Here your raise to game is not particularly sound. However, there are the usual two good reasons for mentioning the diamonds. Partner will be able to judge the fit if the opener bids 4♠. He will also know what to lead if the opponents do buy the contract.

F. You should bid 4♣. Since you are a passed hand, partner will realise that you are showing a raise in diamonds that includes a good club side suit. You are making a high-level fit bid, in fact. Even if you were not a passed hand, many partnerships would assume that 4♣ agreed diamonds here.